STEPHEN GATELY

GATELY

AND BOYZONE

BLOOD BROTHERS

STEPHEN GATELY
AND BOYZONE
BLOOD BROTHERS

EMILY
HERBERT

JOHN BLAKE

Published by John Blake Publishing Ltd,
3 Bramber Court, 2 Bramber Road,
London W14 9PB, England

www.johnblakepublishing.co.uk

First published in paperback in 2010

ISBN: 978 1 84454 939 9

British Library Cataloguing-in-Publication Data:

A catalogue record for this book is available from the British
Library.

Design by www.envydesign.co.uk

Printed in Great Britain by CPI Bookmarque Croydon CR0 4TD

3 5 7 9 10 8 6 4

Papers used by John Blake Publishing are natural, recyclable
products made from wood grown in sustainable forests. The
manufacturing processes conform to the environmental regulations
of the country of origin.

Contents

CHAPTER ONE

DEATH IN MAJORCA

A t first glance, the news was just unbelievable: Stephen Gately of the hugely successful Irish boy band Boyzone was dead. Reports were flooding out of Majorca, where Stephen and his civil partner Andrew Cowles owned a holiday home, that the singer had simply keeled over in the night: staggeringly, the news turned out to be true. He was found dead at 1.45pm on Saturday, 10 October 2009, on the sofa in his luxury apartment in Port Andratx, aged just 33. What could possibly have happened?

It was a shock for many other reasons, too. Not only was Stephen far too young to have passed away, but he was also one of the most popular stars Ireland has ever produced and had just enjoyed a new lease of professional life with the reunion of Boyzone in 2008.

It seemed just the blink of an eye since Stephen originally hit the big time with Boyzone's cover version of The Osmonds' hit single 'Love Me For A Reason' – how could this have come to pass?

On top of that, just a decade earlier, he'd made show-business history when he became the first ever member of a boy band to openly admit to being gay. He might have been forced into the declaration through concerns that he was about to be blackmailed, but the wave of public support that followed – and endured – was a revelation as to quite how far times had changed from just a few years previously, when such an admission might well have destroyed his career.

In the first hours and days after Stephen's body was found, intensive and lurid speculation began to emerge as to what had been behind it all, although the Spanish police were adamant from the very start that there were no suspicious circumstances and no hint of criminality. 'There was no suicide note or evidence of any drug use or excessive drinking, and the dead man's friends were at a loss to explain what had happened,' said a source close to the Spanish police. 'All we know so far is that they had gone out the night before till late and had quite a few drinks and raised the alert when they found Stephen dead.'

Solicitor and friend of the Gately family Gerald Kean also spoke out. 'There's no drugs involved and it's not suicide,' he remarked. 'There is nothing untoward; it's not drugs, we don't believe, it's not suicide, it's not murder, it's not a fight. That's what we've been told.'

Meanwhile, as the news began to spread, people were shocked to the core. 'David and I are stunned by this tragedy,' said the pop legend Elton John, who with his partner David Furnish had introduced Stephen and Andrew. 'Stephen was the gentlest, kindest soul. We send our love and condolences to his partner, Andy, and to all his friends everywhere.'

Louis Walsh, the *X-Factor* judge who discovered Stephen and had been Boyzone's manager, described himself as 'absolutely devastated' and in 'complete shock'. Indeed, he was so upset by the news that he was forced to cancel an appearance on *The X Factor*, which was due to be filmed that night.

Producer Simon Cowell added to the general sorrow. 'I want to say on behalf of the show, this is really, really tragic news and I want to send our condolences to the family,' he said. 'Our thoughts are with Louis, who is obviously not here tonight. They were incredibly close. But, as they say, the show goes on.'

Even Bertie Ahern, the former Irish prime minister, was moved to speak. 'The Gatelys are in my own constituency,' he said. 'I know the family, I knew Stephen. He was 33 years of age, 15 at the top, a fine musician – it's just a huge tragedy to Irish entertainment, Irish music and further afield as well.'

The four remaining members of Boyzone – Ronan Keating, Keith Duffy, Mikey Graham and Shane Lynch – were beside themselves. They released a statement paying tribute to Stephen, who they called 'Our friend and brother.'

'We have shared such wonderful times together over the years and were all looking forward to sharing many more. Stephen was a beautiful person, both in body and spirit. Our love and sympathy go out to Andrew and Stephen's family. We will love you and miss you forever, Steo.'

With that, they flew out to Majorca to give Andrew their support. 'We just need to get over to where he's passed and work out what we need to do,' said Shane.

Take That, the English boy band with whom Boyzone had enjoyed an amicable rivalry in the mid-1990s, were also shocked and spoke of Stephen's tragic passing. 'Our thoughts and prayers go out to Andrew and Stephen's family, friends and band mates,' they wrote on their website.

Indeed, everyone wanted their say. 'He was loveable and sweet-natured and will be hugely missed,' Stephen Fry wrote on Twitter.

'This wasn't supposed to happen,' said Paul Gambaccini. 'This was not in the script.'

But what had really happened? Slowly, details began to emerge. Another man had been at the apartment that night, a Bulgarian called Georgi Dochev, 25. Indeed, it was Georgi who found Stephen's body: he had met Stephen and Andrew in the Black Cat nightclub in Palma the night before.

'Stephen was there with Andrew when I arrived at 3am and they were still there when I left at around 5.45am,' recalled a fellow reveller. 'They weren't off their faces, but they were drinking. They weren't being rowdy – they were just two lads on a night out. Andrew was dancing and Stephen was jigging around. People went up and chatted to them, but it was all very low key.'

Georgi had come back to spend the night with the couple, which gave rise to more lurid speculation about what had gone on. Initially there was speculation that Stephen might have choked on his own vomit, but that turned out to be incorrect, although the trio certainly had been drinking heavily earlier that night.

Gerald Kean, who had become the family's de facto spokesman, was keen to set the record straight before the official inquest began. He rejected suggestions that Stephen had been on an eight-hour drinking binge: 'I think all the information that we have would indicate natural causes,' he said on ITV1's *This Morning*. 'We would certainly hope to get answers following the post mortem.'

Others were also keen to refute suggestions that Stephen and Andrew regularly overdid it. 'Stephen and Andy were regulars here over the summer,' said a waitress at the nearby The Gran Follies Beach Club. 'They were very polite. We knew Stephen was a singer, but he was very modest. They would often come here for a beer or two, but I wouldn't say they were heavy drinkers.'

Certainly, it seemed very odd. 'He was in a strange position,' recalled a police investigator, describing the scene. 'He was found squatting down on the sofa almost in a praying position. His partner was beside himself with grief and was being comforted in the couple's bedroom by a neighbour who he'd called on to help.'

The apartment remained shuttered, while Andrew could not bring himself to appear publicly or to speak to the press. By now, the rest of Boyzone had arrived and they were driven to their old friend's apartment in a Mercedes people carrier, then taken inside without saying anything to the press. However, at other points, they could scarcely contain themselves in their grief: it emerged that Ronan Keating had been running a marathon in Chicago when he heard the news. 'I'm absolutely devastated,' he said. 'I can't believe it's real. Stephen was loved by every one of us. He was one of the most caring, compassionate and gentle people I've ever known.'

Stephen's body was taken to Palma's Institute of Forensic Medicine and an autopsy was to be carried out, although this was delayed for a day as it coincided with a bank holiday in Spain. Standard practice was followed: an investigating judge was assigned to the case, while the formal identification of the body by relatives would not take place until the autopsy had been done.

Georgi Dochev now spoke out, keen to stem the more lurid speculation that was mounting. 'I found the body – he was very white and cold,' he said. 'I discovered the body and the image still haunts me; I've barely slept since. I found Stephen dead and I woke his husband. I am still really upset. It is simply not true that I ran from the flat or that I am a suspect. I spoke to the police all of yesterday to tell them what I know.'

Georgi's English wasn't very good, but clearly he was extremely taken aback by the tragic turn of events. 'I was the one who called the ambulance because Andy was too upset,' he continued. 'It's awful, I am in shock and I cannot sleep for days; it is really upsetting. I have only known him for a while. I was with the husband all day on Sunday and I have talked to the police, but I cannot speak of other things. I am still nervous and really upset.'

As for what had happened immediately beforehand, Georgi didn't want to talk about it. 'This is not something that I want to… I will forgive this [sic]' he said. 'He talk about. Andy and I have been forgiven by the police but I don't want to say anything else without checking first with him.'

Although Stephen's body would have to remain in Majorca until the autopsy, plans were now being made to bring him back to Ireland for the burial.

'It was Stephen's wishes to be buried in Ireland and, after all they've been through together, his band mates want to make sure it happens as soon as possible,' said a source close to Boyzone. 'Stephen's family are desperate to have him home so they can grieve properly. Ronan and the boys volunteered to head over to Majorca to personally oversee arrangements. They've done so much together over the years and travelled all over the world touring. Stephen always loved touching down on a plane in Ireland. They know it is what he would have wanted, to have them at his side when he arrived in the country that he loved for the final time.'

The pair had actually been planning a quiet night in

and had only decided to go out at the very last minute.

'I spoke to them on the Saturday evening and they said they were just going to chill out at home,' revealed a neighbour. 'Stephen said he was tired and on a health kick, so he was staying off alcohol on his holiday. Something obviously happened to change their minds. I saw them leaving later in the evening and they were in good spirits. Stephen was holding Andy's hand as they left the apartment and got into a car.'

Andy, unsurprisingly, had fallen to pieces. Deeply shocked by what had happened, he continued to blame himself, although it would soon become apparent that there was nothing he could have done.

'I will never forgive myself for this,' he told the other members of Boyzone. 'He died and I couldn't help him. I feel like my life is over.'

'They kept telling Andy that he shouldn't blame himself, but he just kept crying his eyes out,' said a source close to the band. 'The guy is in a deep state of shock and he hasn't slept for a minute since this tragedy unfolded. He is a total mess and everyone is worried about him. They told him that there is nothing he could have done and that he has to stop blaming himself.'

But Andrew wasn't the only person that Stephen had been involved with who was shocked by events.

Eloy de Jong had been involved with the singer when he had first come out as gay in 1999. Not unnaturally, he was stunned by what had happened and even went so far as to ring him after he knew of the death just to hear Stephen's voice one last time.

'I rang him and it went to voicemail, but I didn't get his voice,' he said. 'He didn't have a message set up. I wanted to hear him just one last time.'

Indeed, Eloy, who was also a pop star (a member of a boy band called Caught In The Act), had been with Stephen through some very difficult times. 'I remember it being so difficult to let our guard down because we were not yet openly gay,' he said. 'Ronan used to help us keep things quiet. We had to be clever about the way we hid our relationship.'

And of course, he was there when Stephen became the first ever member of a boy band to announce that he was gay. 'We agreed we wouldn't let anyone blackmail us and we made the decision to tell everyone, because Stephen was in love with me and we felt it was right,' Eloy continued. 'Afterwards, it was such a relief for him.'

The two lived together for a while, in Eloy's home near Amsterdam. 'Those were great years,' he recalled. 'We had a canal boat and used to just leave our mobiles behind, leave all the madness and go on the boat. We loved cooking together. He never ate enough vegetables, so I would make him eat his greens. He used to sing and dance in front of me. He was so talented.'

And Eloy was another to defend his former lover against accusations of excessive behaviour. 'Stephen was never a big drinker,' he said. 'People think that because we were both pop stars we would be taking drugs and drinking all the time, but it wasn't like that. Stephen wasn't like that at all. The final time I spoke to Stephen was last year. He rang me for a catch-up. I can't believe we'll never speak again. It's so sad – he was so young, I'll never forget him.'

On 13 October, the first real indication of what had happened came out when the initial results of a post mortem were announced. It transpired that Stephen had a rare heart condition, that he himself had not been aware of, and had thus succumbed to Sudden Adult Death Syndrome (SADS), a rare condition which claims 12 men a week in Britain. He had suffered a pulmonary oedema, an accumulation of fluid on the lungs.

'His lungs have been waterlogged very suddenly, suggesting the heart had failed,' announced Dr Sanjay Sharma, an authority on the subject. 'That is a heart attack. In young people like Stephen, the vast majority of heart attacks are due to either hereditary diseases affecting the heart muscle itself, or an electrical fault of the heart. If I was a betting man, I would say it was an electrical fault. The heart would go into a fatally fast rhythm, around 300 beats a minute. That would only need to happen for a couple of minutes to cause death. Often in these cases, the first symptom is death.'

That, at least, put rest to rumours that Stephen had choked on his own vomit. A court source also backed up the theory. 'Stephen's death has nothing to do with any alcohol he drank that night and it has nothing to do with drugs,' he said. 'I'm not saying Stephen didn't vomit, but I can categorically state he did not choke on it.'

It did emerge that Stephen had been smoking cannabis on the night of his death, but the fact did not appear to have had any bearing on what occurred.

Given that it was clear by now that death was from natural causes, this also meant that Stephen's family would soon be able to take their loved one home. 'The family desperately want Stephen to be back in Ireland where he belongs,' revealed a family friend. 'They were shocked by the results. The band had regular medicals when they toured and he was generally clean living, fit and healthy. They take comfort that Stephen died in a house he loved, near someone who loved him, and may simply have fallen asleep and not woken up.'

But that was not entirely an end to the affair: full results were expected in an announcement in November. However, enough information had been released to quell the more lurid rumours, as well as to allow the proper funeral arrangements to be made.

'There were no signs of violence,' said a court spokesman. 'The judge has authorised Stephen's family to take his body back home. The court will wait for definite results of tests from Barcelona. While they wait, the investigation is open. Stephen's husband has [been] declared as a witness. The judge will take statements from the other witness present. If all these steps confirm natural causes, the case will be closed.'

As matters began to calm down, Louis Walsh went on the Irish TV network RTE, where he reminisced about his friend and protégé. 'We're all in shock,' he said sadly. 'Nobody can believe it – the guys, me, nobody. We are in shock. The boys are devastated. It's like they have lost their very, very best friend – and me, too. His best friend was his sister Michelle. I don't know how she is coping. The boys are like his family now. The four boys were like four daddies for him.'

Stephen started out from a very humble background to ascend to the dizzy heights of fame. 'He came from Sheriff Street,' Louis recalled. 'He was a very working-class kid. All he wanted to do was sing and go to the West End, and he loved Disney, that was Stephen. Of all the people I've worked with, I don't think anybody thanked me as much as Stephen. He used to always say to me, "If I wasn't in Boyzone, I don't know where I'd be today, thank you." A great, great, great professional kid.'

And Louis also recalled how worried Stephen had been in the early days of his fame, before he officially came out. 'He lived in fear,' he admitted. 'He lived in absolute fear of the media and the media outed him in the end, but it was a fantastic reaction. There was no negativity. He loved to go out and party and have a good time, but he was very, very good living. He was a one-off. All Stephen lived for was to be singing music. I think he was the glue in the band, because he kept everyone happy.'

Stephen also took a good deal of interest in his mentor's work on *The X Factor*. Talking to another interviewer, Louis revealed, 'He used to text me during *X Factor*, telling me who he liked and who he didn't. We had some incredible nights out in London; we'd always go somewhere fabulous. We'd gossip, have fun, fall around being silly – he was so happy. The band had never been in a better place. I have never seen a band so close. We were always having a laugh, always. Stephen would send me funny texts. He was like a child, wanting to be loved.'

Indeed, the pair had met up only a week previously, full of plans for the future.

'I wanted him to do *Celebrity Big Brother*,' said Louis. 'He said he'd think about it, but he didn't want to do it. He wanted to be in the musical *Jersey Boys*. He told me, "That's all I want."'

If nothing else, the results of the post mortem began to clear up the mystery, not least because it emerged there was a history of heart disease in the Gately family.

'As soon as I heard he had died, I knew it was a heart problem,' Stephen's mother Margaret told family solicitor Gerald Kean. 'It has lifted a huge burden off our family's shoulders.'

Kean went on to elaborate: 'Margaret felt all along Stephen died from a heart-related problem. There is a heart condition on his dad Martin's side of the family. The whole family are now going to get themselves checked out after this in case they have the same problem Stephen's had. He would have no idea he had this condition.'

One particularly sad aspect of the whole affair was that Stephen appeared to be so happy and settled shortly before he died. Indeed, he and Andrew were even thinking of starting a family of their own.

'I think I won't be truly complete until I have children,' he revealed in an interview shortly before he died. 'That would be my biggest dream. I'd truly love to be a dad. Andrew and I have talked about it and how it would really fulfil us. It's definitely something I want in the future. I've seen the joy it has brought my Boyzone band mates and how much happiness their children bring them. I pray all the time. I have little conversations with God as I'm walking around in everyday life. There's definitely a bigger picture for us all.'

And the relationship with Andrew was happy and settled, too. 'We are just a regular couple and we love nothing more than sitting in front of the TV with a bottle of wine and a takeaway, and watching *The X Factor*,' he said. 'I live for being on the stage. Being back with the lads from the band is just a dream come true. They are my brothers.'

The other members of Boyzone had by then left Majorca, but they returned to the island on 16 October once more to escort the body of their former band mate home. Stephen's funeral was to be held in the St Laurence O'Toole Church in Dublin, close to where he grew up.

It was at this point, however, just before the funeral was due to take place, that a massive furore erupted, which threatened to overshadow the whole sad affair. Writing in the *Daily Mail*, the columnist Jan Moir produced a piece with the headline THERE WAS

NOTHING 'NATURAL' ABOUT STEPHEN GATELY'S DEATH.
She went on to write that the circumstances
surrounding his demise were 'more than a little sleazy'
and that, 'under the carapace of glittering, hedonistic
celebrity, the ooze of a very different and more
dangerous lifestyle has seeped out for all to see'. Moir
also compared his death to the recent suicide of Kevin
McGee, the former civil partner of *Little Britain* star
Matt Lucas.

The uproar was immediate. Moir was accused of
homophobia, which she vigorously denied, while
complaints began flooding in to the Press Complaints
Commission. The article had also appeared online:
Marks & Spencer promptly demanded that an adjacent
advertisement for the store be removed from the site.

Moir herself was called upon to explain her words:
'When I wrote that "He would want to set an
example to any impressionable young men who may
want to emulate what they might see as his
glamorous routine," I was referring to the drugs and
the casual invitation extended to a stranger,' she said.
'Not to the fact of his homosexuality. In writing that
"It strikes another blow to the happy-ever-after myth
of civil partnerships," I was suggesting that civil
partnerships – the introduction of which I am on the
record as supporting – have proved to be just as
problematic as marriages.'

But the uproar was on such a huge scale that it surprised some people. Almost immediately, six separate Facebook groups appeared, demanding the *Mail* retract the article and get rid of Moir; the newspaper, meanwhile, changed the online headline to read: A STRANGE, LONELY AND TROUBLING DEATH. The Twitter community went into overdrive, in some cases actually posting Moir's address, while prominent Tweeters, including Stephen Fry and illusionist Derren Brown, expressed their disgust. Even Bertie Ahern felt prompted to have his say: 'You could see it last Sunday and Monday when I was in London and some of the papers were waiting to write some sensationalist piece about him. The guy was a good guy, who died of natural causes. I can never understand why people don't just leave things simple.'

With such a row going on in the background, culminating in 23,000 complaints to the Press Complaints Commission, it might have been easy to forget that a funeral was about to take place, but, on 16 October, the remaining members of Boyzone arrived back in Dublin, accompanying Stephen's coffin. The lads took his body to the church themselves and kept a vigil the night before he was buried: as a friend said, Stephen did not like to be left alone. They shared fish and chips, and a bottle of wine. 'We all had great peace of mind until one of us started to snore – he knows who he is,' said Keith.

But Andrew was finding it harder to cope. The night before the funeral, there was a viewing of Stephen's body, but, when the casket was opened so everyone who loved him could go in to say a goodbye, he almost collapsed.

'He looked completely peaceful, asleep and beautiful,' said a friend. 'It was hard for all concerned, a heartbreaking moment. But for Andrew, who – remember – found him and tried to save him, it was more than he could stand. His knees just gave way and he collapsed, and the boys literally had to hold him up.'

A red silk handkerchief was placed in Stephen's pocket – his favourite colour – and, the next day, the boys all wore something red in his honour.

The funeral itself was deeply affecting, with the church decked out with pictures of Stephen throughout the years, while lilies and candles were placed everywhere. Thousands of mourners, celebrities and the local community lined the streets: Louis Walsh, David Furnish, Westlife and Jason Donovan were there, along with Andrew, of course, and Stephen's family. Messages of condolence were also sent in from Sir Elton John, George Michael, Robbie Williams, Take That, U2, Simon Cowell, the Beckhams and Cheryl Cole.

Ultimately, the service, conducted by Father Declan Blake, was both a sombre affair and a celebration of Stephen's life. The most poignant moment came when a distraught Ronan paid tribute to his old band mate: 'Steo loved to laugh and, by God, we did laugh,' he began. 'He had the oddest sense of humour on the planet. If he were here right now, he'd say, "Ro, I'm looking for a stained-glass window. If you see one around, let me know."'

Ronan was clearly very moved: his voice was trembling and his hands were shaking. 'The world has lost one of its brightest stars,' he continued. 'We have lost our brother and I have lost my wingman. He will live on in our songs and, whenever the four of us are together, he is alive. We will carry on, but it will never be the same without him. A beautiful man, who is now the perfect angel – forever young, but never forgotten. A brother and a son, a husband and a hero – I'm going to miss you, brother, love you, always will, but we know you've found peace, perfect peace.'

The band took it in turns to share their memories of Stephen, or Steo, as they called him. He was a 'giant of a man', said Keith Duffy, adding that Stephen always worried at auditions that he was too short. 'We never knew how tall Stephen actually was and I don't think he knew, either.'

Ronan, who also sang 'In This Life' and 'Happiness',

revealed how Stephen had given his band mates women's names: 'Keith was Kitty, Shane was Shanice, Mikey was Mikeala and I was Rosaline,' he said. 'Of course, he was Stephanie.'

Keith and Mikey both said how brave Stephen had been to come out as gay. 'After four years and tremendous courage, Stephen became a pioneer in showing young people it was OK to stand up to who you were and what you believe in,' said Keith. 'So many owed him so much for what he did.'

Mikey mentioned Andrew 'who helped Steo blossom into the man he always believed he could be'.

Shane Lynch was much too overcome to speak, but embraced the others to give them his support.

Louis Walsh was present, but also far too upset to speak. Instead, he released a statement: 'We have to celebrate his life. He would absolutely love what was happening here today. I keep expecting him to just turn up with a big grin on his face and deliver a cheeky wisecrack. I know Stephen wouldn't want us to mourn for him, but it is going to take all of us some time to get over the shock of losing someone we all loved so much.'

David Furnish, who, along with his partner Elton John, was also very moved, told how Elton had been left 'completely bereft' by Stephen's death, adding,

'He was like a ray of sunshine – there was not a bad bone in his body. He was one of the kindest and most uncomplicated people.'

Afterwards, the Irish cabaret singer Tony Kenny sang 'Alleluiah' and Mikey read a Prayer of the Faithful.

When the service was over, Stephen's coffin, a pine casket decorated with a gold crucifix, was carried out to a hearse: it was adorned with the words 'Our Brother, Our Son' and transported to Glasnevin Crematorium.

Stephen was dressed in a typical Boyzone sharp suit and his trademark red trainers – together, Andrew and Margaret had chosen what he should wear.

Afterwards, Margaret described how she felt about her child: 'He was a wonderful son – nobody can understand how proud I am of him. Today was a testament to Stephen that he'd made an impression on the world and won't be forgotten. He would have been deeply proud of the turn-out on the streets where he grew up. It was a rough area, but he never fell into a bad crowd. I hope I brought him up properly and people can realise how amazing he actually was.'

And as for Stephen being gay – 'It wasn't a big deal,' she said. 'I knew he was gay and it wasn't a problem. The Lord invites everyone into his group and we were all fully behind him. I loved him no matter what.'

Contrary to some speculation, in Stephen's mother's eyes, Andrew was a member of the Gately family and so he would remain. 'I'm going to love Andrew and be there for him,' Margaret declared. 'He's one of the family – Stephen loved him with all his heart and he made my son happy. I asked Stephen when they got together if it was love and he said it was more than anything he'd ever found.'

CHAPTER TWO

A DUBLIN CHILDHOOD

It was 17 March 1976. Martin and Margaret Gately, who lived in Dublin's tough, working-class Sheriff Street area, were beside themselves with delight. Margaret had just given birth to her fourth child, a boy called Stephen Patrick David, born in the Rotunda Maternity Hospital in Dublin. Mark, Alan and his sister Michelle were already in situ and Margaret would go on to have one more child, Tony.

The Gatelys were a typical Irish working-class family. Growing up, they were all close and, although they lived in a rough area, it was a source of pride to Margaret that they never got into trouble. And Stephen, in particular, was to turn into a charismatic little boy. Though shy throughout his life, once he was performing – which he started doing when he was very young – energy radiated out of him. From early on, it was clear the family had a special little boy.

The new arrival brought joy to the family, an adorable child who would grow up to be the apple of his parents' – and Michelle's – eye. But life for the Gatelys was not easy back then. Martin was a decorator, Margaret worked as a part-time cleaner and money was tight. 'My dad used to be a painter and decorator, which was a nightmare for me, because sometimes I had to go to work with him, for a pound a day, and scrape about 20 walls,' Stephen revealed in later years. 'But my dad kind of taught me, and that was nice. And my mum was a full-time mum, except she used to do a spot of cleaning.'

All five Gately children shared one room; for a time, Michelle and Stephen even shared a bed.

'I view it as an experience,' Stephen once said. 'We had great fun in that little bedroom. There was pipes going across and we would scale them to see who could get around the wall the quickest. We didn't have money so we made our own amusement.'

But he was never able to put posters up on the walls – his older brothers had already bagged all the available space with pictures of Bruce Lee.

From very early on, Stephen and Michelle formed a particular bond, one that would endure right up until Stephen's death at such a tragically early age. Like so many large working-class families, Margaret found she had too much on her plate to deal with all of them, and so care of the younger children was farmed out to the older ones – and it was particularly obvious that it should be Michelle's role, as she was not only close to her little brother, but also the only girl. So Michelle became not just a sister, but also a parental figure – although without the same strictness of a parent. The two absolutely doted on one another, and they always would.

'My mum was quite busy with the five of us, so she always used to get me to mind Stephen,' Michelle later recalled. 'I'd take him and Tony out. Mum would be looking out of the window, keeping an eye on us at all times. He was a good kid: a very smiley, good-humoured child. He was always happy until you did something wrong – like the boys took one of his toys – then he'd sulk. But Stephen never made a big fuss. He was a soft child, a lot softer than the rest of us. I always thought I had to look after him more than the others. If the boys were ganging up on Stephen, I'd protect him.'

It was a bond that would never break.

As an adult, Stephen was to gain a reputation for being the quiet one of Boyzone and so it was when he was still a child. He was a dreamer, who could sit quietly amid the frenetic goings-on all around him; even in a very small flat packed with his family, he had an ability to set himself apart that would stay with him for the rest of his life. 'I was very quiet and introverted,' he remembered. 'I'd never say anything to anybody – I just sat in the corner. I'd sit at the window of our flat for hours, watching as if it were TV.'

And, when he did venture forth, it was more often than not in the company of his big sister. Stephen was never downright reclusive, but he did like Michelle to be present, whatever he did, and so he would turn to her when making any plans.

'There were five shops near by, and right beside them was a big tree with a shrine to Mary, where people could sit and pray,' he recalled. 'I'd always be asking Michelle, "Could we go and see Mary?" She'd take me and we'd sit down, put our money in and light a candle.'

But he was certainly always very quiet. Michelle also remembered him being withdrawn when he was quite young, but then suddenly able to start playing up to the people around him. It was a very good description of how he would be in Boyzone: bashful one moment, then capable of holding the attention of millions the next.

'Stephen was amazingly shy as a little boy,' said Michelle. 'At around six, he started coming out of his shell a little, then all of a sudden at eight he became a completely different person – a lot more determined than the rest of us. He always did well in school. The teachers doted on him because he was a cute little kid, and he worked hard.'

Stephen was also a team player, someone who took part in school activities, particularly theatricals. Of course, this would be the making of him in later years. But he was always reflective, another trait he maintained into adulthood. 'I was into life and scenery and snowfalls,' he once said. 'I would sit wrapped in a duvet, watching the rain. I still like to. It costs nothing to walk around a park or read a book.'

Indeed, he had an almost dreamy quality, the soul of a poet. It was to be no surprise when he ended up making a career in the Arts.

But Stephen certainly had a silly side, as well. When he was seven, he walked into a joke shop in Dublin's Camden Street and poured a bottle of invisible ink over himself, in the full expectation that it would make him disappear. Naturally, it did not. In fact, his earliest ambition was to be a wizard, with J. R. R. Tolkien's *Lord of the Rings* being one of his favourite books. His earliest exposure to music came via the family's scratchy old record player. Stephen would listen to Whitney Houston and Madonna; blues records belonging to his mother, too, opened up another, very different world.

And the bond with Michelle merely strengthened as

time went on. The two played together when they were alone and would be sent out to do the weekly shop, quite a responsibility in itself. 'Michelle and I got groceries for my mam every week,' Stephen explained. 'From when I was around 12, I never used a trolley. I'd say, "That's for grannies." So I'd lug the bags, two on each shoulder and one hanging from each arm. Once a bottle of washing-up liquid burst – we were so upset and scared. Not having much money, letting something get spoiled was just something you didn't do. After that, we'd wrap the washing-up liquid in at least two bags, so that, if it burst, we'd be OK.'

Michelle also remembered those shopping trips as being something of a bone of contention. 'I'd go off shopping for my mum and I'd always drag Stephen along to help,' she said. 'He didn't like it one bit and we often rowed about it. So there were bad times as well, but never anything serious. Neither of us can stay angry for long – we'd always end up laughing.'

Stephen initially attended St Laurence O'Toole's school, which describes itself as a 'small, friendly docklands school situated in the centre of the Dublin's Docklands area'. Among much else, the school offered many after-hours clubs, with varied activities for the pupils to take part in. Stephen settled in well, made friends and began to work out where his interests lay.

Back with his parents, there might not have been

much money, but it was a warm, comfortable home. There was great jollity in the evenings: Martin would have a pint of stout and sing Irish ballads, while Margaret played the spoons, displaying a talent for entertainment that clearly ran in the family. And they did, at least, have a television set.

'I was the remote control,' Stephen remembered. '"Get up and change the channel", "Change the channel", "Change the channel"... Also, I was the tea maker. I don't know how many cups of tea I've made in my life. You know what people are like in Ireland, they just drink so much tea.'

He also looked back on his childhood fare with much affection: it was usually mash, mince flavoured with Oxo cubes and sometimes a dish along the lines of pig's trotters: 'They were gorgeous! I don't eat red meat any more, but I would love a pig's foot. I remember Saturday night sitting down, watching TV, sucking on a pig's toe.'

But, while Martin and Margaret were loving parents, they were also strict. Living in a rough area, there was plenty of scope for the growing family to land themselves in trouble, but the couple would have none of it.

'Our parents really kept an eye on us,' said Stephen. 'They didn't want any of us getting into trouble; they did a good job. People come up to them and say, "How did you raise such a lovely family?" It was discipline – we had a lot of respect for our parents. If they said, "Don't do that," we didn't do it.'

Indeed, the possibilities for going off the rails were all around. Dublin had an increasing problem with drugs and it would have been all too easy to get sucked into that particular mire, either in search of some form of escape or a quick buck. But somehow, like the other members of Boyzone, all of whom came from equally poor backgrounds, they managed to evade the temptations and grew up in a totally respectable manner. His steady upbringing would stand the adult Stephen in good stead. At the time, there were also fights between the residents of the different blocks of flats, St Bridget's and St Laurence's, mainly between the children, but 'some of the adults would probably end up fighting as well'.

It was a poor area, although Stephen would express irritation in later years when it was described as a slum, with a strong community spirit. 'I have lots of fond memories of growing up in Dublin,' he said in one interview. 'I had a happy childhood, with a very close family. I seem to remember spending a lot of time hanging out in the playground in Sheriff Street, near where I used to live. There was a boys' playground with slides and a girls' playground with swings. We had a football pitch too. I grew up in a close community and

I remember once a year we'd have a community week, where there were competitions for things like snooker, darts and fancy dress. All the kids would queue up and they'd hand us out a packet of crisps, some sweets and a drink each.'

He did, however, remember much darker aspects too. 'When I was a kid we were living in Sheriff Street flats, and there was this ghost of a man who used to come out,' he said. 'I used to see him all the time, and I'd scream. I was around four when I saw him for the first time walking around the flat, and he used to come out every night. [But] I had a happy childhood, not too much darkness at all. Not that I was spoiled because I was a pretty boy or anything like it, at home or at school. I get my downs, but they don't last long.'

From an early age, Stephen was also beginning to display some of the traits that would lead him to the very top of the show-business tree. For a start, he had the performing gene, but, perhaps just as importantly, he possessed perseverance, patience and determination. When he wanted something, he went all out to get it, and, although he and the other members of Boyzone would go on to find success relatively quickly, for the first year they would need every bit of determination they had.

Circumstances made them all pretty inventive and practical, too. Growing up, Stephen and his friends had to earn money any way they could: at one stage chopping up wooden pallets into kindling and selling them for 10p a bag.

'I think most people bought them because they thought, Aw, God love them, out there in the freezing cold,' he remembered.

At other times, they would spend the day bagging potatoes for a bar of chocolate, a Coke and a packet of crisps. He did not, however, complain about this, saying, 'There was a lot of poverty and crime. It was a tough and rough area, but nice people and good community spirit.'

In stark contrast with the life that he would one day lead, Stephen was used to doing without, so much so that even his shoes were worn down.

'I know what it's like to have no money,' he told one interviewer years later, when he'd become famous. 'I remember having to wear a pair of shoes to school which had a couple of holes in them – they were stuffed with cardboard so the rain wouldn't get in. To this day, I love buying myself new shoes. I'll never get fed up with that!'

His school had no uniform, which meant that Stephen stood out all the more: in fact, he used to wish there was a uniform just so that he could blend in.

Unsurprisingly, there was no money for anything like a holiday, which Margaret minded far more than her children ever did. Indeed, Stephen remembered her weeping when they couldn't afford to send him on a school trip, although there were sometimes excursions elsewhere. 'Our holidays, for summer, were being sent to our aunt's house, or else it was this big place, this huge house, 300 kids, with these dormitories... All the kids from the area went and it was your holiday. It was brilliant.'

On another occasion, he recalled, 'We never had holidays; we just used to hang around together. Or have treats like the cinema or winkle-picking on the beach. We used to boil the winkles and sell them on the street.' He was never ashamed of all this in later life, unlike so many stars who try to create a very different image of their previous lives to the reality. 'I am proud that I have succeeded, but I am also proud that I have some stories from my childhood that are very different to the way I live now.'

And there were deprivations. Christmas, especially, could be a difficult time: 'Christmas was always tough and Dad, who is a decorator, used to do lots of work around that time to make sure that money was OK for the presents,' said Stephen. 'My parents did whatever they could and were brilliant, but I didn't want to live like that forever. I didn't want to scrape through, always having to get certain foods and brands because they were cheaper. There were always lots of stolen things going around the doors of the houses in our street and we would buy two for the price of one. I have lots of happy memories but, when I grew up, I wanted more.'

His parents also became highly adept at avoiding their children's requests by saying that the asked-for present was far too heavy for Santa to carry. But they all accepted this and the stark contrast between then and the later years, when Stephen had a great deal of money and could give some of it to his family, was even more marked. And he always had an ambiguous attitude towards material wealth: although he was happy to have it and would, in adulthood, acquire large properties with the rest of them, he never gave the impression that this was all that motivated him. His parents had brought him up to see what really mattered in life.

There was something brewing away in Stephen, though, which surfaced when he was still very young. 'When he was 12, he asked for singing and dancing lessons,' Michelle later recalled. 'I don't know where it came from – maybe something he saw on TV. Our mother and father were really supportive but nobody we knew had done singing or dancing before. My folks had to ask him, "Where do we go?"

'So he found the place and they let him go, and right away he did really well at it. I don't ever remember Stephen singing at home. It was just so quick – suddenly, he wanted to do the dancing and singing, and he was so good they asked him to teach the younger children at the community centre after school.'

By this time, he was attending North Strand Technical College. He was not particularly academic, but began to excel at some sports and increasingly discovered a talent for drama. And his ability to entertain displayed an unexpected confidence, one that would shortly be put to good use. Stephen was slight, as a child as well as an adult, but he never allowed himself to be pushed about. 'We had a good schooling, even though it was very tough,' he admitted. 'I got kicked around a couple of times when I was 14, but that was it. I stood up to the biggest guy in our class, had a fight and kind of got the better of him. After that, if there was a fight going on, I got left out.'

Although it was to be years before he came out, Stephen knew from very early on that he was gay. 'I had a couple of dates with girls when I was at school, but, by the time I was 15, I knew that wasn't what I wanted,' he said. 'I'm sure some of the other kids noticed that, and that I was different, but I'd won the fights, stood up to the bullies, so I never got any bother about it.'

At home, however, his family had no idea of his

sexuality. Michelle, who remained close to her brother throughout his entire life, might have suspected something, but, as far as the others were concerned, Stephen was simply a little bit gauche and shy. Certainly, the fact that he was still tiny, with a shock of blond hair, might have explained why he didn't have a girlfriend, and then there was the fact that this was Dublin in the late 1980s. It was all very much stricter back then, but that was the background the boys came from; the background against which Stephen would one day be forced to admit to being gay.

Although many people don't find it easy to accept their homosexuality, especially when they are younger, matters were complicated by the fact that Stephen was, and remained, a practising Catholic, and of course Ireland happened to be an extremely Catholic country. Many others in similar circumstances have been wracked by guilt, but for some reason this never seems to have been the case in Stephen's life.

'Never,' he once said. 'I've never thought that God would come down and say that I can't do this or that. I went to church and sang at Christmas mass, but I stopped going because I couldn't sit there, bored out of my head, for an hour. God forgives everything. I read a book called *Conversations With God* by Neil

Walsh, which explained a lot of things. This is the only life I have, and, in a hundred years' time, who'll give a shit?'

By his early teens, he was beginning to show a marked talent for entertaining. He landed the lead role in his school's production of *Joseph and the Amazing Technicolor Dreamcoat* (a role he was to play again as an adult), and went on to join Dublin's Gaiety Theatre Group and also taught drama at the local youth centre. Another role was in *Juno and the Paycock*, the second play of Sean O'Casey's Dublin Trilogy. At this time, he started to direct short plays and choreograph dance routines; he also joined a 12-strong disco dance troupe called Black Magic, which won the all-Ireland Disco Dance finals when Stephen was 13.

The experience also proved rather remunerative. 'It was dancing I loved – I would go to a teenage disco every Friday night and take over the whole dance-floor,' he reminisced. 'I went to classes and eventually a friend and I took them and charged the children 50p each. Mum was very proud of my dancing and would get me to perform little routines in our living room when she had friends round.'

But there was no calculation behind any of this: Stephen was doing it because he genuinely wanted to dance. 'It wasn't about getting out of Sheriff Street,' he said simply. 'I just wanted to dance.' He considered himself to be a real-life version of the musical *Billy Elliot*, the story of the young boy from a miner's town, who went on to become a dancer: 'The rough area,' he pointed out. 'They had a miners' strike. We had a bin strike!' Indeed, he went on to sing the title track of the film version in 2000, but had no clue that such greatness awaited him. Back in those days, the height of aspiration was to dance at Butlins – which he did every Wednesday afternoon.

Stephen knew something else from a young age, too: that he fully intended to become famous. 'From when I was around 14, I practised my autograph,' he admitted in 1999. 'All the boys at school would laugh. About two years ago, two of the guys in my class passed me by in town. I stopped to chat and one said, "I remember you sitting in class signing autographs – they'd be worth something now!"'

And his acting skills were beginning to pay off. Stephen and his mother Margaret actually appeared in Alan Parker's wildly popular 1991 movie *The Commitments*, albeit for just a second: they can be seen at the start, haggling for goods in a market. 'I did a little piece in *The Commitments*, but blink and you'll miss me,' he said in later years. 'Literally, I'm gone. I was like 14 and they got about 300 kids from my area, and we got £20 for doing it.'

Another film appearance almost followed: Stephen

also filmed a blink-and-you'll-miss-it slot in *In The Name Of The Father* (1993), starring Daniel Day-Lewis as a small-time Belfast thief, wrongly implicated in the IRA bombing of a pub, based on the story of the Guildford Four. He and various other youths were filmed throwing bricks from a rooftop: in the end, alas, the footage ended up on the cutting-room floor.

But, in fact, Stephen was turning into something of a prodigy. He was a good-looking boy, and so, from the age of 14, he began a brief career as a model, having signed up with Dublin's International Modelling agency. Assignments included modelling clothes for some major department stores, as well as weekly visits to Butlins to take part in fashion shows and dance routines. As he was rather small, he couldn't take on every assignment, but did enough to get himself noticed – a fellow model and friend was the young Colin Farrell, who would also go on to do great things. At the same time, he supplemented his earnings with a job at Makulla's clothes store.

When he was 16, he moved to Assets model agency, and at around the same time started to sing karaoke. Indeed, it was because of his modelling that he himself discovered for the first time quite what a good voice he had. 'I was on a coach travelling to one of the modelling assignments I used to do as a teenager,' he later recalled. 'We all used to sing on the coach and one day an agent asked if there was anyone who could sing, and everyone chorused, "Stephen can!" I had no idea my voice was good, and, to this day, I've never had a singing lesson.'

But the episode gave him ideas. 'I always knew I wanted to do something in the entertainment industry when I left school, but it wasn't something I was pushed into. I loved drama and dancing at school and I would always be the first one who'd get up in front of the class to do some acting. I had a good drama teacher who encouraged me, but I think a lot of my teachers thought I should stick my head in books and concentrate on studying, so I'd get a good job when I left school.

'My ambition was to be successful doing something to do with music – not necessarily being famous. Coming from a poor family, I didn't want to have to worry about money when I was older. I had a dream and I wasn't going to let anyone take that away from me.'

CHAPTER THREE

TAKE *WHAT?*

In 1989, UK music manager Nigel Martin-Smith, who had witnessed the meteoric rise of a new young band in the US (New Kids On The Block), had been inspired to put together a singing outfit of his own. He held auditions and ultimately created a five-strong outfit called Take That.

After beginnings that have been subsequently slightly glossed over in the gay clubs of Manchester, Take That burst on to the scene to become one of the most successful bands of the 1990s (and, in a later incarnation, of the Noughties), winning awards, gaining millions of teeny-bop followers and, most importantly of all, bringing a serious amount of money into the bank.

By 1993, Irish music manager Louis Walsh, who

had been watching the astonishing rise of the boy band – even that term was new back then – was beginning to think that an Irish version of Take That might just work. Louis, born on 5 August 1952 in Kiltimagh, County Mayo, was also of the view that he was the man to do it, for he had already launched another hugely successful act, Johnny Logan, in 1980. Logan went on to win the Eurovision Song Contest, singing in front of 500 million TV viewers (a feat he was to repeat twice more, making him the person who has won the most Eurovisions since the contest began). Following this success, Louis strongly believed that, with the right people, he might just be able to put together a rival for Take That.

And so, in mid-1993, advertisements were placed in the Irish press for auditions to form a new boy band. At the same time, in a completely unrelated chain of events, a football player called Mark Walton had broken his ankle, and, while convalescing, he, too, began to think that the time was right for an Irish boy band. He mentioned this idea to his closest friend, who replied, 'Yeah, why not? I'll give it a go.' That friend was Shane Lynch, a student of architecture.

The only problem was that neither man had the faintest idea how to go about it, so, when they saw Louis Walsh's ads in the papers, they were delighted. Auditions were to be held in Dublin's The Ormond

Centre in November 1993. Well over 100 people applied; they were asked to sing 'Careless Whisper' by George Michael and 50 were called back. They included Shane and Mark, Stephen, Mikey, Ronan and Richard Rock, the son of the hugely successful Irish entertainer Dickie Rock. Then working as a mechanic, Keith Duffy was not in the initial bunch of hopefuls, but Louis spotted him dancing at a POD nightclub and asked him to attend.

For the second audition, the boys were asked to choose their own numbers: Mikey sang 'Two Out Of Three Ain't Bad' by Meat Loaf, Keith went for Right Said Fred's 'I'm Too Sexy' and Ronan opted for 'Father and Son' by Cat Stevens. All got through apart from Mikey: in its very first incarnation, Boyzone was to have a line-up of six.

Stephen, unsurprisingly, had been nervous, but determined as well. 'When he got the first interview, he asked me, "Do you think I'll get in?"' Michelle recalled. 'But mostly it was like, "I am getting this." I remember meeting him for a coffee and Stephen saying, "It's down to the last 50 people." He was pretty confident. Then he was down to 20.

'My parents wanted him to get it, but didn't really know what was going on. When he did, it was brilliant – there's been nothing like it in Ireland. The family was very shocked.'

'When I auditioned for Boyzone I was confident because it was something I really wanted and I thought, Right, I'm going to do this,' Stephen later remembered. 'And I went in there and I danced, and I sang George Michael's "Careless Whisper", Lionel Richie's "Hello" and "Right Here Waiting" by Richard Marx.'

In fact, Stephen had to do four auditions in total, more than any of the others, but eventually he got through.

On 18 November 1993, Boyzone was officially formed.

But there were various teething problems that took a while to sort out. Ronan Keating's family were not happy: he had been due to travel to New York to study on a sports scholarship, with a view to competing in the Olympics in the athletics category. It was only because his sister, Linda, supported him that he finally decided to try his luck with Boyzone.

'It was an agonising decision,' he admitted afterwards. 'Running had always been my first love and I lived for it, but I also liked music. I started playing guitar when I was ten and, while I was at school, I'd been in various bands. When the chance came up with Boyzone, I had to go for it. At first, my mum said there was no way I was throwing away all I'd done on the track for a dream, but, in the end, it was my decision. Everyone thought I was mad, dropping running, but we soon had a massive chart hit in Ireland and England. That answered anyone's doubts.'

Keith Duffy's family was none too pleased, either. But Louis, in marked contrast to some managers who take advantage of their charges, urged all the boys to seek proper legal advice, which went some way towards calming down their anxious parents. All were now signed up.

Louis now put the boys through vocal training and had them signed up with various local clubs to start getting some experience, but then came an incident which made him decide he had to be in far greater control of his young charges. Shane and Keith were in Shane's black Golf GTI when Keith revved up to 110mph, before slowing down to 90mph to take a corner. The two were lucky they weren't killed: the vehicle hit the kerb, flipped over and spun round in the air several times before landing on its roof. Miraculously, the boys were barely injured and were found hanging by their seatbelts. Following this incident, a furious Louis read them the riot act and got them to sign much tighter contracts. He was now very much in control.

The six-part outfit, still with Mark Walton and Richie Rock but without Mikey Graham yet, was now intact. However, it was another seeming disaster that finally got them on their way: the boys appeared on Ireland's *The Late, Late Show*, but Mark and Richie's performances were deemed to be beyond the pale. Following this, they were ejected from the band.

Not everyone realised how badly the two had done: Michelle, still reeling from the news that her little brother Stephen might be about to hit the big time, watched in slack-jawed amazement: 'The first thing that happened after he got in Boyzone was *The Late, Late Show*, which is a big thing in Ireland,' she said. 'They'd only come up with a name for the band that day, and Gay Byrne asked, could he have them on the show. They'd barely met and they had to perform together on a live show.

'I got a phone call from Stephen an hour before, saying he was going to be on it. I was at the airport, so I couldn't watch it with my family. It felt so strange. I was so proud, and I was so nervous for him, just hoping it would go off all right. They all did a great job, and it was like, "Wow!" I was very, very surprised – I hadn't known he was that natural.'

But that was not what everyone else thought. The band was so bad, with such a poorly rehearsed routine, that they had the audience laughing (and not in a good way). Also, Shane managed to upset various people by grabbing his crotch.

Gay Byrne was unimpressed. 'These lads have decided to cash in on a particular market,' he declared. 'There's no talent whatsoever. Nothing. They don't sing, they don't write music and they don't play instruments.'

It was hardly an auspicious start.

'I'm glad we made some people laugh,' said Ronan, much later on. 'We cringe when we see it. I can laugh now because I was successful, but, if I hadn't been, I'd cry. I would, I'd cry!'

Louis, however, realised that the line-up was wrong, and so Mark and Richie were asked to leave – there had been other problems, too, such as the boys not turning up for rehearsals. Richie was also working as a DJ, which was raising eyebrows, and there was a final showdown when he missed a gig. After a huge row, Louis let him go. Mikey was called in and Boyzone, as it was in its heyday, was on its way.

Unsurprisingly, given what was to happen to the band, Richie was pretty bitter about it all. He went on to become an established DJ, but developed problems with drink and drugs. 'Being sacked from Boyzone has ruined my life,' he said in an interview in 1999. 'I'm a shadow of my former self. At first, it was like all my dreams had come true, the moment I'd been waiting for all my life. My father Dickie

Rock was an entertainer and all I'd ever wanted to do was write songs and perform. Everything fitted. But, looking back, I should have seen the warning signs from the beginning.'

The way he told it was very melodramatic, but who could blame him? He'd been offered the opportunity of a lifetime and it had gone badly wrong. And it got worse: 'Six of us were chosen for the final audition,' he continued. 'There was me, Ronan, Stephen, Keith, Shane and another lad called Mark Walton. We broke off for lunch and, when we came back, Mark had gone. He had disappeared. No one knew what had happened, and no one dared to ask. It was as though he had been erased from history.'

Richie didn't immediately follow: instead, along with the rest of them, he began rehearsals – which Louis claimed he frequently missed.

'We recorded three songs and had loads of photo-shoots to perfect our image. We were always rehearsing and we were slowly being groomed to become the biggest band to come out of Ireland since U2. But there was a flipside to the band: the management ruled it strictly, and Ronan and the lads were always terrified about losing their places. You had to conform.'

Realising, of course, the opportunities that lay ahead, the other boys did just that. Meanwhile,

Richie, much to Louis's dismay, started clubbing. Plus, there were other differences between Richie and the other members of the band in that they were all working-class and from the north of Dublin, whereas middle-class Richie was from a different area.

As far as Richie is concerned, the real problem began when Louis brought John Reynolds, a nightclub owner, on board to co-manage the band. According to him, Reynolds was even more unhappy about his clubbing than Louis: 'Then one day I was one hour late for a meeting with Louis and the lads in a bar. When I arrived, Louis … told me I was sacked. The next day it dawned on me – I had been deprived of the biggest chance of my life. I rang Louis in desperation, but he never returned my calls.'

And very soon it was brought home to him exactly what he had lost, and, although it is skipping ahead of the story, this is how he perceived the next few years. The boys brought Mikey on board, signed to Polygram and, not long afterwards, they were on their way. But for Richie, things couldn't have been tougher. 'It drove me insane,' he admitted. 'I ripped the posters I had on my wall and threw out the scrapbook of photos I had with the band. If they came on telly while I was watching with my mum and dad, I would go mad and make them turn it off. Then I'd run upstairs, and switch it back on again and watch it in silence with the volume turned down. That's when I started taking drugs to block out the pain. At first, it was ecstasy and loads of alcohol. Then I got into heroin and I was doing up to £200 worth in a day. If I was desperate, I would go to my doctor for methadone.'

But matters became even worse. Richie and Keith bumped into one another at a Robbie Williams' concert and had a long chat afterwards, 'Keith apologised for what had happened and he promised that, if they made it really big, he would take me with him and sort me out,' said Richie. 'I was writing songs of my own and he told me that he would help me. But nothing ever happened and we never got in touch – it was just talk.'

He did, however, decide that he had to turn his life around. 'I checked into a rehab clinic and have been off heroin since, and I've started to write songs with my new group, Lectrosoul. I'm not asking for money or sympathy from Boyzone now, just a bit of acknowledgement that I existed.

'I remember walking through Dublin city centre after I'd been given the boot – I was moping because I was still very depressed. I remember I stopped in the middle of the street to light a cigarette and looked up. Lo and behold, there was a huge billboard advertising Boyzone. My heart sank and I had a very hollow feeling in my stomach. I could have dropped dead there and then. It was as though God was torturing me. I went home to drown my sorrows, but I switched on the telly and there they were on *The Late, Late Show*, singing the single. I couldn't believe it. Anger welled up inside me ... I hoped I would just wake up and it would all be a bad dream.'

But it wasn't and he was only too aware of quite how wrong it had gone. 'The bitter irony was that *The Late, Late Show* was the only-ever TV appearance I had made with Boyzone,' he said. 'It's even worse because we were a disaster on it. I remember once turning on the radio and one of their songs came on. I changed to another station and then another one of their songs came on. When I am walking down the street, people recognise me and some of them come up and offer me sympathy and encouragement. It is like someone has died. But I like it because it gives me hope.'

Nor did his parentage help. Richie's father was himself a phenomenally successful performer, and so he had that example before him all the time. 'It's hard trying to live up to my dad,' he admitted. 'All I ever wanted to do was be like him. My dad has been very good – he's offered me encouragement and said words to the effect of, "That's show business, son." He said it may be a blessing in disguise and a test of my character. If I don't find success as a songwriter, then the Boyzone saga will haunt me like a ghost for the rest of my life.'

When the story came out, however, Louis Walsh was robust in his own defence. 'I sacked him because he was unprofessional,' he said. He was too much of a risk and that's why he went; the rest is history. When I found out who his dad was, I thought he would have been a lot more professional. He is from a very nice family and I don't know why he behaved like he did.'

Mark Walton, on the other hand, was nothing like as bitter about the past. He returned to school to complete his education and then persevered in making a return to show business, going on to join another band, Fifth Ave. Another five-piece outfit, which went on to have a limited degree of success, this was not a boy band: the other singers were Beverley O'Sullivan, Danny Cummings, Jessica Molloy and Terry Gaynor, while their manager was Mark Murphy.

'This time I'm ready for the big time,' said Mark, in an interview in 2001. 'Although I was one of the original members of Boyzone, I left before they signed their record deal. I don't think I was ready for it mentally then, but I know I am now. We've put in a lot of work over the last two years, writing and practising. And, although I used to regret not following Boyzone through to the end, I don't any more because I'm doing something that I love and I know Fifth Ave are going to make it.'

Truth be told, they did to a small degree, but it was nothing like the acclaim that was awaiting Boyzone.

And, ironically, the success they did achieve came from another outfit. Westlife (who they supported on tour) were also managed by Louis Walsh. 'We played a gig at The Point and a gig in Belfast's Odyssey Arena,' Mark continued. 'Obviously, because we were performing in front of such huge audiences we were a bit nervous, but, once we got on stage, we really enjoyed ourselves – it was such a huge buzz. The Westlife lads were great, really supportive of what we were doing.'

Back at the end of 1993, it was still not clear if and when Boyzone would make their breakthrough. Some of the boys still had jobs on the side – Stephen at Makulla's clothes shop, Ronan was working at Korky's shoe shop, while Shane was at his father's garage – because they certainly weren't earning any wages from the band. Meanwhile, Louis did indeed bring John Reynolds on board. This turned out to be a wise move for Reynolds was very au fait with the Irish music industry, as he owned the POD clubs in Dublin. From then on, the two split the work: Louis focused on the day-to-day running of the group, while John looked after the business side.

And it helped that the boys all got on. Although they had not been friends as such, Stephen had been aware of Ronan for years. 'I knew him beforehand, but I never really talked to him,' he recalled. 'He worked in a shoe shop, and I used to go into town a lot, so I knew who he was.'

Indeed, Ronan wondered why it had taken them so long to meet up. 'It was strange that we'd never met because I used to see him all the time,' he remembered.

But they quickly became firm friends. 'He's got a brilliant head on his shoulders,' Stephen said of Ronan in an early interview. 'He's very bright, very intelligent, but funny at the same time. We're best buddies, it's a gas.'

Although he was now edging closer than ever to the limelight, Stephen continued to retain his quiet side. Asked what got on Ronan's nerves, he replied, 'Me not talking. I can get really quiet at times and not talk to anyone – I get upset and don't speak to him, and he goes mad, saying, "Tell me what's wrong!" I'm not that private, but everyone has to have their peaceful moments.'

Ronan himself backed that up. 'Yeah, he does keep quiet a lot,' he said. 'That's just him, though, and everyone has to do that sometimes.'

Above all else, though, the two just clicked. Asked what they had in common, Stephen replied, 'An awful lot of things! We think the same way – we're both designer-labels men when it comes to clothes! We've both got three brothers and one sister. You'd be surprised how much we had in common.'

The first months of 1994 were a struggle. 'We played to near-empty halls and people flicked cigarette butts at us,' Ronan later recalled. 'We were a laughing stock in some quarters, but it was important not to be put off. We reminded ourselves we were the ones on stage and carried on singing. We used to call some gigs "The Doorstep Tour" because often the stage was literally the size of a doorstep. We'd travel only to discover the nightclub was the extension of somebody's house.'

Mikey too had similar memories. 'We played the backside of nowhere with 50 people there,' he said. 'We went through it all, but we kept going and came out on top. We danced on tables – we played places where the wind doesn't even blow. But that's what you have to do; we realised that, if we captured 10 fans, it was worth it.'

But their luck was about to change: Louis managed to get the boys signed to Polygram Ireland in a deal for three singles and possibly an album, should the singles do well enough. Everyone involved was keen to seize the moment and therefore moved fast: within a month they had released their first single, 'Working My Way

Back To You' (previously a hit for both the Four Seasons and the Detroit Spinners), with Stephen and Mikey on vocals. Ronan appeared on the B-side, singing 'Father And Son'.

And it worked. Boyzone were not destined to spend years, as Take That had done, working the pubs and clubs before anyone noticed there was a new band on the scene: almost immediately, success was theirs. The single got to No. 3 in the Irish charts and so overwhelming was the attention and resulting publicity that the boys who were in jobs had to leave them almost overnight – apart from anything else, with the demands of the group on their hands, they no longer had time to do anything else.

Boyzone worked hard on promoting their material in Ireland before flying to London to see how they would be received in the British capital. The answer was well: more promotional work and appearances followed, and, while they were in the UK, they recorded what was to be their breakthrough – a cover of The Osmonds' single 'Love Me For A Reason'. This went to No. 1 in Ireland and No. 2 in Britain. The boys had arrived.

There was, however, one final mountain to climb. Despite their obvious talent, Boyzone were initially written off in the music press as just another manufactured boy band, with nothing to show for

Stephen Gately's funeral took place in his hometown of Dublin, Ireland on 17 October, 2009.

Above left: Hundreds of fans gather outside St Laurence O'Toole Church to listen to the funeral mass over loudspeakers.

Above right: The churchyard was lined with flowers placed in tribute to the beloved singer.

Below: Ronan Keating, Mikey Graham, Tony Gately and Shane Lynch carry Stephen's coffin.

Above: Stephen's parents Margaret and Martin Gately mourn the loss of their son.

Below: Keith Duffy, Ronan Keating, and Mark Plunkett stand together.

Above left: Louis Walsh, who described Stephen as his 'very, very best friend', arrives at the church.

Above right: Stephen's partner, Andrew Cowles, with the support of a friend.

Below left: A fan's loving tribute.

Below right: David Furnish attends the funeral.

A fresh-faced Stephen Gately joined Boyzone in 1993 after replying to Louis Walsh's advertisement looking for singers to form an 'Irish Take That'.

At the height of their success, Boyzone were one of the biggest-selling artists in the music industry. All three of their studio albums reached number 1 on the UK Album chart.

Above: Boyzone in 1994: Ronan Keating, Mikey Graham, Stephen Gately, Shane Lynch and Keith Duffy.

Below: (*L-r*) Stephen, Mikey, Shane, Keith and Ronan.

Above: Ronan Keating, Stephen Gately and the rest of Boyzone join the Dunblane Choir in making a charity record.

Below: Boyzone performing at the Slamas Awards in 1996.

Above: Stephen Gately launched his solo single 'New Beginning' in 2000.

Below: In 2002, he took the lead role in the West End production of *Joseph and the Amazing Technicolour Dreamcoat*.

Gately made his pantomime debut as Dandini in *Cinderella* at the Churchill Theatre, Bromley.

themselves. Particular criticism came from the fact that they had released two cover songs, rather than writing their own material, and so there was some active debate as to what would be released next. The record company wanted another cover version, but the boys were adamant: this time it would have to be their own work.

And so, 'Key To My Life', written by Stephen, Ronan and Mikey, was their next release. When it, too, reached No. 1 in Ireland and No. 3 in Britain, this was the vindication the band needed that audiences loved them for who they really were. Clearly, after that, an album was on the cards, and so came the release of *Said and Done* in 1995. It featured seven covers and six original numbers. They were on their way.

Stephen's life, like the rest of Boyzone, was turned upside down in a trice. Almost overnight, they had gone from total anonymity to real fame and the contrast between living the lives of ordinary Dubliners to being pursued by screaming fans wherever they went was immense. But they had to get used to their new existence – and fast.

'I've basically had to give up my whole life!' admitted Stephen in one interview. 'I can't go out and I used to enjoy that a lot. I can't meet my friends; I have to run everywhere to get away from girls!

I can't walk down the street, I have to take taxis everywhere!'

Ah – girls. Stephen was in a boy band now, with vast numbers of young female fans eager to latch on to his every word. And they adored him. Each Boyzone member had his own specific fan club, who bought his records and secretly hoped that one day they might meet their idol, that he would take a fancy to him and then – who knows? Stephen knew this and he understood what was expected of him: back then, there was simply no way that he could have told the truth about himself.

And so, in his earliest interviews, he is rarely allowed to get away from the subject of girls. Did he miss having a girlfriend? 'I do in a way, but I don't really have the time,' said Stephen. 'I could make the time – I'm waiting right now for a nice person to come along. If she comes along, I might just say yeah! We've not really got any rules like Take That to say we can't have girlfriends; it's just a matter of time. It definitely wouldn't work out because of work, though. We know ourselves, without being told, that business and pleasure don't mix. We get a little advice to keep us on the right track, too.'

Had he ever been in love? 'I can't remember,' he said. 'I think I have, but she couldn't have meant that much if I can't remember her! Maybe I haven't met anyone I've loved properly, yet. I don't fall in love very often. Usually within the first week I know if I'm in love – and, if I'm not, it's over! You know you're in love because you feel like being with the person 24 hours a day. I'd do anything for someone I loved.'

So, what did he look for in a girl? 'I look for someone who doesn't lie and who likes being themselves,' said Stephen gravely. 'Someone who isn't afraid to show themselves and not put up a front to me; basically, a real, natural down-to-earth person. I always go for older people – everyone I've been out with has been older and they've told me I'm very sussed for my age. All my friends say that, too.'

Was he romantic? 'Yes, I buy flowers and chocolates when I go out with a girl,' he said. 'I'd also buy meals and do romantic things for my girlfriend, if I had one.'

And how would he describe himself in a lonely hearts? 'Don't go out with me! I'm a bit of a laugh. I like doing mad things – I'm a bit wild. I like going out on the town, I love the cinema and I'm fun to be with. That's about it, really!'

The 'Don't go out with me!' certainly rang true, but the fact is that Stephen had no choice but to go along with it all. Reading those comments now, it's hard to escape the note of terror at the back of it all – how on earth was he supposed to describe his perfect woman? Or his romantic gestures, or indeed, what he looked for in a girl? But at that early stage, although the rest of Boyzone already knew the truth, there was no way that he could be open about his homosexuality. It had simply never been done before by anyone in his position.

But there was much, much more where this came from. His best snog? 'A couple of years ago, but I'm not telling you who she was. A good snog is when it's slow, as if someone really cares for you.' Ideal woman? 'Michelle Pfeiffer.' So, which pop star did he fancy? 'Wouldn't you like to know! But Louise from Eternal and Baby out of Reel 2 Real, 'cause they're both really sexy!'

Interviews from those early days also reveal a kind of innocence in starting out in the world of show business. The downside of it all, said Stephen, was the very early mornings and he professed admiration for PJ and Duncan – one of the earlier manifestations of Ant and Dec.

Girls featured heavily in everything he said. In an interview in 1995, when he was still only 19, he reflected on what had happened to him: 'I was a schoolboy with hardly any experience of life when I got this job out of nowhere. Suddenly, everything changed, and it was a shock. I realised what it was like to be famous because I couldn't walk down the street without getting mobbed. If I went shopping on my own, it was like risking my life, because huge gangs of girls would surround me, asking for kisses and an autograph.'

Indeed, as anyone who has walked into sudden fame will testify, it can be as terrifying as it is exhilarating. It's no surprise that so many of the young and newly famous fly off the rails.

Then there was a joint interview that he gave with Ronan, in which the two revealed what they thought about each other: did Stephen have any secrets? 'Not at all!' said Ronan. 'Definitely not!' Had they ever fallen out over a girl? 'No, and we never will!' [That, at least, was spot on.] 'We have pretty similar taste, except he likes dark-haired girls and I prefer blondes.' Will you be mates in 10 years? 'Yeah, I think we will.' What Ronan couldn't even imagine, of course, was that, in 14 years' time, he would be giving a eulogy and singing at his friend's funeral. It would have been unthinkable, back then.

But no one was really concerned about Stephen's homosexuality (apart, perhaps, from Stephen himself) for they all had much bigger fish to fry. Louis's strategy had worked: now they were fully fledged rivals to Take That, with an enormous fan base and a big future ahead. Indeed, Boyzone were one of the biggest success stories to come out of Ireland in decades – five young men with looks, talent, charisma and all to play for. None of them was from a rich background, but now that too would change, with great wealth and privilege rolling in. In all, it was quite a time that lay in wait for them.

CHAPTER FOUR

LIFE IN THE LIMELIGHT

In early 1995, it became obvious that the boys were going to have to spend far more time in London, and so the decision was made to move them, *en masse*, to live in a house together. Naturally, this had pros and cons. On the plus side, it meant that they were all there to support one another, no bad thing as this was the first time that any of them had been away from home. However, it also meant they were cooped up and the stresses and strains could take their toll. In public, they were becoming internationally famous pop stars, while in private they were having silly squabbles about domestic strife.

Ronan, by now the *de facto* leader of the band, once told a story redolent of the way they were living, when they nearly came to blows over a packet of cornflakes. 'There just wasn't enough food to go around and the early mornings were getting us down,' he admitted. 'But you just have to get on with it and put the bad times behind you, because the good times were far, far outweighing them. When we moved into the house in London, it was the first time most of us had been away from our parents. We were given £100 for the housekeeping, which we spent down the supermarket, although we probably bought far too many biscuits and cakes.

'But it was the state of the house that eventually got to us the most. You should have seen what a tip we'd turned it into after just three weeks living there! We never did any housework. I think the washing-up only got done twice. There were takeaway cartons all over the place, mixed in with smelly socks and clothes everywhere. I was ashamed to invite anyone in. It was a complete dump by the time we moved out. It's probably better that we stay in hotels in the future.'

Despite those protestations of domestic squalor, the boys were on a roll. They won the 1994 *Smash Hits* award for Best Newcomers – 'Love Me For A Reason' had shifted over 700,000 copies in the UK alone. Stephen could hardly believe it was all happening. 'The success of the record has been just brilliant,' he said. 'It's such a high when you go on shows alongside

East 17 and Take That. But we haven't got two pennies to rub together; it makes us laugh when we go home and everyone says we must be millionaires. We won't see any money for a long time. We're lucky we've got some clothes sponsorships that put shirts on our backs. We get treated very well – all our food, accommodation and travel are paid for. It's just that we've hardly got a fiver to buy a round of drinks for each other.'

But they were all in it for the longer term, now. As previously related, the boys understood the importance of writing their own music (which also meant they would earn more, as they would receive royalties for the songs) and Stephen was more than happy to talk about that, too.

'We have started writing songs ourselves, which we're performing to fans and are growing in confidence every day,' he said. 'We're working very hard on making this group the biggest that we can. My ultimate dream is to buy a big house on the millionaire belt outside Dublin where the stars live. I was out there recently, looking at the flash houses and thought, Gosh, imagine living there, right next to where Bono from U2 has his place! I'm just keeping my fingers crossed that in ten years' time I might be able to do it.'

In reality, it was to take nothing like that long.

Until then, Take That had been reigning champions in the boy-band stakes, but now there was a feeling that they had become all too blasé. Boyzone were on the verge of snatching their crown. It is hard to remember that, in later years, Take That did implode: after Robbie Williams left, which he was to do later that year, the remaining four would endure years of musical exile before getting their second bite of the cherry. That time around, of course, they did not take their success for granted and appreciated the fact that they had been given a second chance. Indeed, ironically, it was their successful reunion that was to inspire Boyzone to regroup.

But, back in 1995, Take That were a little jaded whereas Boyzone were raring to go. 'Take That have already reached the pinnacle of their success,' declared Ronan. 'There is not much further that they can go. They've been around for five years and I think they now want out of the teeny-bopper scene. We are younger and hungry for success, and we are appealing to the new breed of 12- and 13-year-olds.' (That was certainly true – Ronan was just 17 at the time.)

Keith, relatively ancient at 20, backed that up. 'There are a lot of fed-up fans, who have stopped following Take That because they say they are now out of touch and out of reach,' he said. 'They say that

Take That don't sign autographs or say hello any more. Once they did, now they go to their cars.'

And just in case the point hadn't already been made, Shane chipped in. 'They've got too big for their boots,' he insisted. 'They've made their money and they're getting lazy. And they are not very friendly to us. We can chat to East 17, Eternal and Michelle Gayle on a one-to-one level, but Take That seem to look down on you. Even so, I think they are great performers. I just don't like their personalities.'

That was to change, of course, when Take That were humbled but this was still to come.

Such had been the speed of Boyzone's meteoric rise that some people were now beginning to compare them to The Commitments, the fictional band from the film of the same name, in which Stephen had fleetingly appeared. Louis Walsh thought so, too.

'You need working-class guys because they want things,' he explained. 'There is a hunger there and they don't mind working for it. I am from a working-class background and so I have that same hunger. I was also looking for guys who want to be pop stars. There were a lot of good-looking boys at the auditions who could not sing and a lot who could sing, but couldn't dance or didn't look good. When Stephen and Ronan sang, I just could not believe it –

they had star quality all over their faces and I knew I had two great singers there.'

Stephen himself was asked how he managed to get through. 'Probably with my singing ability,' he said. 'It came down to a bit of everything – talent, a bit of luck, a bit of confidence, the ability to play or dance and perform. You've got to have looks, talent and an image, so I wouldn't have got it if I didn't have those things.'

True enough, and, although that comment might have appeared a smidge self-satisfied, Stephen was far more modest than he sounded at that point. Really, he felt that he wasn't that good-looking, despite by now having achieved heartthrob status, but why was that?

'It's just the way I was brought up,' he explained. 'Not to be... I don't know... I never thought I'd get to the top. I always hoped I'd be able to get into a group like this, but, when I went to the auditions, there were so many fellas who were looking brilliant and I just thought I had no chance. When I got it, it was amazing.'

By now, the band's popularity was such that they had to set up a fan club, while the first of many rumours about Stephen's love life began, with stories that he was dating the pop star Kelly O'Keefe. He rose above it all, far more concerned about the fact that the band had just written its first song, 'Key To My Life', with the accompanying video to be recorded in a school.

'It wasn't hard for me to play being back in school – I could still be there myself,' admitted Stephen, who shared lead vocals on the number with Ronan. 'But we're very pleased with the results. Myself, Mikey and Ronan wrote this song last August and it goes down a storm every time we play it live. We're very proud of it and we just hope the fans will like it.

'The teacher with the cane [in the video] brought back some bad memories for me. There were times when I dreaded going to school – like when I didn't have my homework done or we had tough exams. It was nice playing the part, but I was glad when filming ended. I have to admit that my last day at school was probably the happiest of my life.'

Rather ironically, in light of later events, eyebrows were raised when it emerged Boyzone were to play at the G.A.Y. club in London's Soho 'They are straight,' said a spokesman for the band. 'I don't know how this gay gig has got out, but it's true they will be playing there. The group has a huge following that includes young female pop fans, as well as the gay community. They are doing this special gig as a thank you to the gay fans who buy their records.'

In public, of course, Stephen was as straight as

the rest of them, although he was also feeling pretty overwhelmed. The attention could sometimes be scary. 'What many people may not realise is that I am from a very ordinary family, where your feet were kept very firmly on the ground,' he once said. 'Then suddenly I started getting girls telling me they wanted to sleep with me and VIPs offering me free bubbly at posh parties. It was then that I realised that that kind of high life was far too daunting for me at my age. I'd much rather a night in with the remote control in one hand and a cup of tea in the other.'

Of course, there may have been more than one reason for this, but even for someone who didn't have to worry about the truth about their private life slipping into the public arena, it was still pretty overwhelming. However, the pressure to keep up appearances continued: when the single 'Key To My Life' and accompanying video appeared, Stephen was called upon to recall his own schoolboy crush.

'My first ever crush was with my schoolteacher,' he said. 'She was 22 and French. I took the class only because she was teaching it. I was about 13 at the time and ended up having to quit French as she drove me crazy.'

An older (but not too old) French mistress is a

classic teen fantasy and that, of course, was exactly what it was.

As hysteria around the boys continued to mount, heavy security was increasingly drafted in. They were putting in promotional appearances all over the place – in newspaper offices, radio and TV stations, London's Oxford Street, and, wherever they went, they were mobbed. Fans just could not get enough of them. As Take That began to step away from the limelight, Boyzone's timing couldn't have been better, although the two groups were still seen as rivals at that stage.

Indeed, in the summer of 1995, when Stephen got to sixth place in *TV Hits* 25 Most Fanciable People poll ('Wow! Great! It's brilliant, but I can't help laughing at things like that – I think it's funny!'), Take That's Mark Owen was still at No. 1. But Stephen was beginning to notice a change in himself: although genuinely shy, he was now so much the focus of attention at all times that he was starting to enjoy a certain confidence that he hadn't had before.

'I tell you, I'm a very, very confident person, but only in the last few years, because I was really shy,' he told one interviewer. 'I'd never do anything, I'd be really quiet and I'd never make any friends. Now, though, I have thousands upon thousands of friends and I'm just so confident! I think I got my confidence from the stage, from acting classes and things like that. I am quite a shy person as well – I don't know, I'm just a weirdo.'

Confused, more like.

In the same interview, it was put to him that he got all the girls. 'That's just because I'm small – loads of girls come up to me after the shows and all they say is, "You're tiny!"' Surely, the interviewer insisted, Stephen must feel guilty as far as the other band members were concerned, with him getting all the girls. 'No, because they get a lot too,' was his earnest reply. 'I'd say it's pretty equal in the group, really – we all get girls who like us. Really, a girl's not just going to go for looks; they're going to go for your personality as well, so it's very important the way you come across.'

Above all, Stephen was coming to terms with his new status: that of fully fledged pop star. It had seemed an incredibly short time since he was just another kid playing on the streets of Dublin, and yet now there he was, one of the most sought-after men in the world. Did he feel any different?

'No, I just see me, a person,' he said. 'I just class myself as an ordinary bloke – all of us do, and I think that's done us a lot of justice. When you do interviews on TV, it shows we're just five normal guys, having a good laugh. When I get stopped in the street and people ask for my autograph, I think, Why? I'm just an ordinary person. Then I have to remind myself that I'm not, I'm in a pop group.

'It just doesn't dawn on me sometimes – you just forget that you're in a pop group. You see, I don't think I'm good-looking. No, seriously, sometimes I get up and think, My god, what do you look like this morning?'

But the fans clearly didn't agree. In August, Boyzone played the National Basketball Arena in Tallaght, when a combination of heat and hysteria had dozens fainting: most were revived with a bucket of cold water, but some were taken to the nearby Our Lady's Children's Hospital in Crumlin, others to St James's Hospital.

Stephen continued to be utterly bemused by his success: 'Space is so tight at my home that my gran sleeps in my bed when I'm not there,' he admitted. 'And we all have to share rooms, anyway. We never even had a phone until recently. I bought a mobile, but I was so shocked when the first bill came to £600 that I got rid of it. It was a terrible waste of money. I haven't got a car because I can't drive – but I wouldn't have one, anyway.

'It's really important to me to save money, I'm not ashamed of that, and I'm not bothered what people think. I don't want to end up like Bros – having earned a fortune and ending up with nothing; I remember where my roots are. And I know what I want to do with my life. My ultimate goal is to be able to afford a mansion next to U2's Bono!'

Indeed, this seemed to be becoming something of an obsession, with mention of Bono's place now coming up all the time.

The group's third single, 'So Good', was released in 1995 and soared up the charts, marred only by the fact that both Mikey and Shane suffered accidents that left them in wheelchairs, with Mikey falling off a horse while Shane suffered after leaping off a wall. Despite the ensuing problems when it came to promotional activities, however, their new album, *Said And Done*, made the top slot in both Ireland and Britain. Stephen, meanwhile, was planning ahead: he had got the acting bug at school and began to investigate possibilities there.

'Once word got around that Steve had worked as an actor, offers flooded in,' said a spokesman for Boyzone. 'He is tempted and may yet take up an offer he feels he can't refuse. He has been offered serious roles in dramas, as well as a few roles which could mean a move to Hollywood. But it won't affect his role in Boyzone: he will either do it as a part-time option, or when the group are on holiday.'

Interestingly, although it was Ronan's decision to

pursue a solo career that would ultimately split the band, this was the first indication that the boys might be looking for solo roles in the future rather than simply sticking together.

That autumn, another shock lay in store: although the band had been marketed as squeaky clean, the reality was somewhat different. Keith announced that he and his girlfriend Lisa Smith were expecting a baby. 'It's been a bit of a shock, but we are very much in love and plan to stay together,' he said. 'Lisa wants to have the baby and, as soon as I finish this tour, we will be making plans for the future. I'm crazy about her.' Indeed, the couple were to go on to marry three years later and have another child, but, even so, this was Catholic Ireland. It was also an indication that, behind the scenes, some of the boys had a sex life.

There were immediate fears that the news might jeopardise various lucrative deals already on the table, but there was no going back now. Louis Walsh was keen to emphasise the positive: 'It seems the fans are delighted at the news,' he said. 'We never intended to keep secret the fact that his girlfriend was pregnant. Anyway, you couldn't hide it for very long, could you? I have a feeling Keith might be getting a lot of baby presents from his many fans in the months to come, particularly when his birthday comes round. Everyone involved with Boyzone is delighted. I know that Shane, Ronan, Steve and Mikey, who all know Lisa well, have been on the telephone to congratulate her.'

In fact, the pregnancy had no bearing whatsoever on the band's popularity and was an early indication that Boyzone fans could take surprising news in their stride.

Of course, what it also meant was that the other boys got even more attention, including Stephen. 'I do tend to get my share of fans but I'm learning to deal with it,' he said a little wearily. 'You get used to girls coming up to you and demanding kisses and an autograph. What still shocks, though, is the ones who are a little bit ruder. They don't seem to have any problem asking you to sleep with them or even have a five-minute sex romp in the nearest loo. That still shocks me because my upbringing was quite strict. Casual sex was definitely not on the menu – and especially not on holy days and Sundays!'

Although it was a close-run thing, and while Ronan would eventually take this particular crown, in the autumn of 1995, it was generally agreed that Stephen was the sexiest member of the band. With his usual politeness, he continued to deflect questions about whether or not he had a girlfriend and kept the emphasis elsewhere instead.

It was also revealed that he had spooky psychic

powers. 'I was really scared when I suddenly discovered that I had these weird psychic powers,' he admitted. 'It's not every day that you wake up and realise you have an understanding of what's going on in other people's lives. But I've tried hard to use my powers carefully and stop them from taking over. It's more about understanding whether people's vibes are good or bad, rather than actually trying to read people's thoughts.'

And he was not the only one with girl-related issues: Ronan had them, too, although in his case for a slightly different reasons. Even so, it could be wearisome to be presented with so much willing female flesh. 'I tell the fans I'm a virgin, and they know to look but not touch,' he said, and, in truth, he was still only 18. 'A one-night stand is not how I plan to lose my virginity. It is a very special thing to me. I come from a good Catholic family and was brought up to respect it. When the girls get fruity, I stand my ground and tell them to wait for the special moment when they know it will be right.'

Like Stephen, he was also having some difficulty in adjusting to his new life. While all the members of Boyzone were only too aware of how lucky they were, at the same time the constant attention could be difficult to deal with, especially from the women. While it is easy to make light of an 18-year-old who is tired of his appeal to women, at the same time, Ronan's beliefs were sincere – he was finding it all a little difficult. He was, however, sufficiently self-aware to appreciate the irony of it all. 'I have everything a guy could want,' he admitted. 'I get to go to places all over the world – we eat out in nice restaurants and stay in lovely hotels. Our records are doing well and we're hoping for high placings in the pop polls, but it seems everybody wants a little piece of me and that can be difficult to cope with – especially when it's girls with sex on their agenda. When you find birds trying to stick their tongues down your throat or groping you in private places, it can get frightening. I get the rudest letters you could ever imagine – from young girls right up to mothers-of-three.'

Poor lad – no wonder he married so young.

Still, the boys had no concerns on the professional front as their careers continued to soar. Their next release, another cover – Cat Stevens's 'Father And Son' – was due and became a smash. As the constant touring and promotion became the norm, Stephen talked of the pressures that he too was under because of the female fans: on the surface, of course, it looked as if he was having exactly the same problems as Ronan. Papers reported, without comment, that he'd never had a girlfriend: it appeared to be just because there was too much pressure and too little time.

'People say I look good, but, to be honest, it makes me cringe,' he said. 'I don't think I have the best face and, more often than not, I blush to the roots if I think a girl fancies me. When I am the centre of attention and dozens of women are staring at me, I just want the ground to swallow me up. Nobody knows this, but I worry all the time. I fret over my complexion, if my hair is OK, whether my clothes fit me, or even what I should say to people.'

But that was nothing compared to what else he had to put up with. 'I've seen down more cleavages than I've had hot dinners,' he continued. 'Girls do tend to come up to me and say saucy things, but I'm just a shy guy who would prefer to get to know them first. Sometimes I get so lonely I have to wipe the tears away. I miss my home, my family, even my teddy bears! I can end up missing my mum so much that I find myself having a cry in my hotel bedroom, but I know that's something I will have to learn to live with.'

Although the money was beginning to come in now, Stephen was still living at home when he was in Ireland. In later years, after he'd come out as being gay, there was a long-standing rift with his parents (mercifully healed before his death), but, back in the early days of Boyzone, he was as close to them as ever. Home might have been modest, but it was home.

'It was my home before I was in Boyzone and will remain my home as long as my family live there,' he said. 'All day and most of the night, a gang of fans wait outside my house for me; I can always rely on it. I usually stop for a chat and to sign autographs. They are so sweet and wait for such a long time to see me. But, once inside, it is my time, that is when I really unwind. I know I will always have my own little bedroom and the 200 teddy bears which I've collected over the years.'

It certainly wasn't going over the top and he was adamant that what made him happiest was sitting in front of a video with a hot meal and a cup of tea. 'I know it doesn't sound very rock 'n' roll, but that chills me out totally,' he said. And of course, there was the strong relationship with his mother – 'She's always there for me when I land back in Dublin after touring the world,' he went on. 'Of course, I dream that one day I shall have my own family and a special girl in my life to settle down with. For the moment, I'll have to be content to snuggle up to my teddies. Winnie the Pooh might not be the most passionate playmate, but at least I am saving myself for Ms Right, whenever she chooses to walk into my life. Until then, I will always be a mummy's boy and proud of it!'

Back then, he was constantly being linked to women too, although, behind the scenes, everyone was well aware of the reality of the situation and it was no secret that he'd never had a girlfriend. Still, the myth was maintained and the latest woman for him to be linked to was Michelle Gayle, actress and pop singer. As a matter of fact, she already had a boyfriend, Sheffield Wednesday striker Mark Bright, but stories continued to circulate about 'secret dates'. And, of course, the public might have been justified in thinking they would have made a perfect match.

In May 1996, Keith became a father when Lisa gave birth to a boy, Jordan, although matters did not run smoothly. Three months after the birth, the couple split, although this proved to be only temporary and another illustration of the pressures they were all under. Mikey, meanwhile, also joined the fathers club: his girlfriend Sharon Keane had just given birth to their daughter, Hannah. In that particular case, the relationship did not survive, but it was all evidence that the boys were growing up. Ronan and Shane had moved to London – a sign that they, too, were beginning to feel the need to break away from what could, at times, be a claustrophobic life.

In hindsight, there were also plenty of clues as to the reality of Stephen's situation. Boyzone raised eyebrows again by performing at another gay gig, the

Astoria in London, shortly after appearing on the National Lottery TV show, and the boys were certainly happy to camp it up. Numbers included the Monkees' old hit 'Daydream Believer', while the openly gay DJ Jeremy Joseph begged Stephen to marry him.

Truth be told, Ronan looked a little out of his depth, but the others were clearly enjoying themselves. 'You lot are awful!' Keith told the adoring crowd.

In October 1996, the boys finally got their first UK No. 1 with the single 'Words'. They were in Germany when they heard the news. 'It's brilliant!' said a delighted Ronan. 'All the lads are just over the moon.'

They were of course, but the pressure certainly wasn't getting any less: Boyzone were forced to cancel an appearance in London's Oxford Street when the waiting 1,000-strong gang of teenage girls got so overexcited that 34 of them had to be treated for hysteria. According to an ambulance man, it was 'utter chaos'.

Meanwhile, Ronan began to regret having been so open about his lack of sexual experience. 'I regret saying that very much,' he admitted. 'Because, whenever it comes out that I'm no longer a virgin, I'm not going to be able to say these things as openly any more.'

Indeed, he'd had to put up with a lot of stick, but then Boyzone had been going strong for years and he was still only 19.

Indeed, if anyone was really suffering at that time, it was Ronan. Boyzone swept the board at that year's Smash Hits Awards, and, in total, the boys won six awards that night, with Ronan voted the World's Most Fanciable Person. But, after the band performed 'Words', Ronan rushed backstage, where he collapsed.

Louis Walsh was quick to calm everyone down: 'Ronan has had a very hectic schedule and had nothing to eat or drink all day,' he said. 'We think he's OK now, but I'll probably give him a day or two off.'

Boyzone would actually carry on as a band for more than three years before Ronan went off to pursue a solo career and the others followed suit, but now the pressures were certainly on. Two of the boys were unmarried fathers, one was an avowed virgin while another was gay and hiding it from the world. Just what would this rollercoaster of a life bring forth next?

CHAPTER FIVE

BOYZONE — OR MENZONE?

By the beginning of 1997, Boyzone's status seemed assured. They were by now one of the biggest-selling bands in the world, having confidently seen off Take That, East 17 and other competitors too numerous to mention: indeed, they were joined on stage by none other than Robbie Williams at a Dublin gig early in the year. Eighteen months earlier, Robbie had left Take That and had gone through a somewhat reclusive phase: he was now beginning to emerge into the public eye once more.

In February, however, there were ructions behind the scenes, with rumours circulating that Ronan was contemplating a solo career. Nothing was being made definite, but it was said that he thought Boyzone should quit while they were ahead – which they certainly were by then. They were untouchable by the competition: the only thing that might have stopped them in their tracks at that stage was a bad accident, which, in fact, they very nearly had. The boys were flying in a private plane across the Australian desert when an engine failed: they were forced to adopt the brace position, while the pilot managed to crash land into the sand. None of them sustained any major injury and they were rescued after eight hours, but it had been a terrifying ordeal. Mikey, in particular, had to be cajoled on to the plane sent out to rescue them.

'They rang me and they were still absolutely petrified,' said Louis Walsh in the wake of the incident. 'Mikey is very upset and says he never wants to fly again. It was very stressful. After landing safely, they had to worry about being stranded in the desert. Fortunately, the pilot was able to give a pretty accurate description of their location.'

The boys had been on location to film a video, and this was duly completed without further mishap. But those split rumours wouldn't go away – both Ronan and Stephen were also said to be interested in acting careers, something that could only have been encouraged when they were asked to come up with a song for the soundtrack of Rowan Atkinson's *Mr Bean* movie. The boys were hoping that it would help them make their breakthrough in the USA, where *Mr Bean* was hugely popular: they had certainly done their bit in the UK. By mid-1997, they'd clocked up two No. 1 albums and eight Top Five hits: by now, they were all financially set up for life.

Meanwhile, Ronan's virginity remained an issue: he continued to give interviews to announce its importance, although he also expressed concerns about being the 'Cliff Richard' of the 1990s. He really was, by now, very much the public face of Boyzone, although Stephen continued to give him a run for his money – if anyone was going to make a successful solo career, clearly it would be one of the two. Ronan, in particular, seemed to be carving out a solo niche for himself: he appeared on Eurovision, putting in a very polished and assured performance that appeared to betoken great things ahead. Stephen, meanwhile, was now being linked to Emma Bunton, aka Baby Spice: while there wasn't a word of truth in the rumour, it certainly did no harm at all to their careers.

And Stephen continued to give the interviews he was required to do, all about looking for The One. 'There's no one special in my life at the moment,' he said. 'I'm always on my own when the rest of the group go to their own hotel rooms. I suppose the day will come when there will be someone, but at the moment I just watch TV.' And of Emma, who in fact had just broken up with her real long-term boyfriend – 'I haven't spoken to her recently.'

The attempt to take on the States continued, with the release of the group's next single, 'Picture Of You', the song that featured on the *Mr Bean* soundtrack. Much to their delight, the boys were able to travel across America on the back of this, although it was a tour of Hard Rock cafes rather than huge stadia: even so, it was a start.

And with the States to conquer, the band didn't look as if it would be splitting just yet. 'Boyzone won't be splitting for at least two years, so I've still got more time to see the rest of the world,' a smiling Stephen said. 'If the time does come for us to go our separate ways, I'll go for a solo career. I'd also love to star in a musical or a film, doing the roles Leonardo DiCaprio does – something like Romeo.' At least a part of that sentiment was to come true.

In early 1998, Ronan's mother Marie died of cancer at the tragically young age of 54. Ronan, himself still only 20, had been very close to her and was stricken by grief. 'I have been walking around like a zombie,' he said afterwards. 'There is a massive gap in my life and I don't know how to handle it. My mother has gone – when I say those words I still can't start to comprehend. It hasn't hit me properly – it's like she is on holiday. Every time the door opens I think it's her with her suitcase. She was my best friend, she gave me everything. I used to ring her every day, wherever I was in the world. I still have the name Mum programmed into my mobile phone and sometimes I still ring it to see if she has really gone.'

He had had a series of girlfriends by this stage and, just before his mother died, he split from the latest, Gabriella Martinez. And, although it would still be some time before he started to carve out a solo career, this may have been the time when the desire to do so really began to take hold. Although it had been mooted a fair few times already, sometimes the loss of a parent finally forces a person into the realisation that they are the adult now, that they had better get on with whatever ambition they want to achieve. Ronan frequently credited his mother with absolutely everything, including keeping him on the straight and narrow, and so her loss was inevitably a severe blow.

Shortly afterwards, his paternal grandmother Annie also died, just adding to the sense of loss. Within the year, he would be married with a family of his own on the way: it is perhaps no surprise that he began to change his life. Barely a month later, he was with a new girlfriend, Yvonne Connolly, the woman he would go on to wed.

The rest of the band was growing up, too. In

February 1998, Shane announced that he was engaged to Easther Bennett (of the band Eternal), with whom he'd had a long-term relationship; the two married a month later, in the Leighs Priory centre, near Chelmsford, Essex. Stephen, behind the scenes, was now together with Eloy.

Professionally, the boys were going from strength to strength, as well: Andrew Lloyd Webber had chosen them to record the number 'No Matter What' from his next musical, *Whistle Down The Wind*.

Ronan's new relationship, however, seemed to be concentrating the mind. For a start, he was already talking about marriage, even though the couple had barely been together for two months. 'Yvonne is definitely the one for me,' he said. 'I have never felt anything like this about anyone else in a relationship before and things are going brilliantly at the moment. We're both busy, but we find time to see each other. Yvonne was a good friend before we became an item and she's been there through my hardest times. She is very special to me.'

Tellingly, marriage wasn't the only change on his mind, though. It was becoming increasingly obvious that he did not see his long-term future with Boyzone. 'It's inevitable that we are going to split up as a band,' he said in a statement that was bound to upset not just Boyzone's fans, but some of the other members of the group, who were nothing like as sure to have a solo career. 'I think, if we do more solo projects, that would help us in the long run,' he went on.

In his defence, Ronan had had to deal with a good deal of loss at that point. Just a few months after losing his mother and grandmother, his 16-year-old cousin Laurinda Clarke died of meningitis. He carried on, but those close to him could sense he was under a terrible strain. There were reports of a collapse and uncontrollable crying fits; when the boys appeared on *Top Of The Pops* to sing their new single, Ronan wasn't there. Louis gave him a bit of time off from the band to recover.

And he certainly used his break to good effect. By now he was 21 and Yvonne 24; the two went on a break to the Caribbean island of Nevis and came back as man and wife. He had met The One, she had supported him through a dreadfully troubled time in his life and, so, why wait? They might have been together for only a short time, but, as Ronan himself pointed out, they'd known one another for years.

He certainly seemed pretty happy about it all on his return. 'I love Yvonne like I thought I could never love anyone,' he declared. 'It's been magic – we're both so happy! Everyone was happy for us. I know we might have disappointed some people, especially our parents, who would have wanted to be there, but we wanted to do this alone together. We wanted a really special, romantic day without any fuss and we decided this was the only way to do it.'

In fact, the pair had been planning it all for several weeks. 'There was no one with us,' Ronan went on. 'It was really private, really beautiful and very simple. It was a day we'll remember for the rest of our lives. We told no one – we knew, if we did, it would all have come out beforehand. It was so hard keeping it a secret, but I am glad we did. I know it seems as if we haven't been going out for very long but we've been best friends for a long time. That really was the foundation for our relationship. We both want children – we love them – but we'll give ourselves a bit of time before we start having children.' He really was moving on.

None of the other boys had a clue about it, as Stephen later recalled. 'I just got a message from him, saying he needed to talk to me urgently,' he said. 'I thought the worst, fearing that something awful had happened. But, when I rang him back, he told me he'd got married and I said, "You're joking!" Then, when they came home, they threw a big party and we all celebrated.'

Of course, one reason why the couple might have chosen to get married as privately as they did was because Marie would have been absent. Ronan's brother Gary was his best man. Ronan himself was all too aware that to many people it might appear that he was subliminally trying to replace Marie with Yvonne.

'I know that's how some people will see it, but that's not the reason I married Yvonne,' he said. 'I married her for the right reason, which is that I love her and she loves me, and I want to be with her for the rest of my life. She didn't just appear from nowhere. We've known each other since I was 10 and she was 13. I was working with my dad, making deliveries to a shop in a little village two doors away from where Yvonne lived. We met and talked, and I really liked her.

'Apart from my mother, she was the first blue-eyed, blonde girl I had ever met in my life who really meant something to me. But just after we met I had to go into hospital for a week and we lost touch until two and a half years ago. Then we became best friends and I realised that I loved her long before I told her. It wasn't until the middle of last year that I knew this was the woman I had been waiting for. Mam knew Yvonne and liked her and, in a way, I believe she set this up. She would have wanted this to be the next step in my life. I still have the rest of my family, but now I have the chance to start a new family: it will be the next chapter in the Keating book.'

But for now, although much change was on the horizon, Boyzone were still going strong. Their next album, *Where We Belong*, released in 1998, was launched in some style, with a warehouse in Chelsea transformed into a funfair for the occasion, before the boys set off on a tour of Europe and Asia.

Keith Duffy was next to tie the knot: to his childhood sweetheart Lisa Smith, whom he wed in Las Vegas in June 1988. Ronan was best man and Stephen was a witness. They were all growing up fast.

The wedding had been a surprise on Keith's part: he'd arranged it without Lisa knowing, although Ronan and Stephen did. 'We were sitting in New York, having dinner, and Keith wasn't himself,' Lisa later recalled. 'I asked him if he was all right, and he kind of played it off, but then he said, "There is something that you should know as everyone else here knows." I looked at him and got a little bit of a fright. Then he got stuck for words and asked Ronan to help. So, Ronan produced a piece of paper with two rings wrapped in it, put them in front of me and said, "You are flying to Las Vegas and you are going to be married there." I couldn't believe it. I cried, and then I laughed and got hysterical and cried again.'

Of course, the couple already had a child together but there was the general feeling that now they had done the right thing. And their reason for getting married in such secrecy was exactly the same as Ronan's and Shane's. 'Unfortunately, the press would kill a wedding in Dublin,' said Keith. 'In the eyes of the Catholic Church, you have to keep the doors open to anyone that wants to come to the ceremony. You can't put anybody on the door, the press have just as much right to be there as anyone else. That's why, when Shane got married, he did it very privately while all his guests were waiting where he was supposed to be married. Then he came in – and because he was already married – locked the doors and put security on.'

Keith, however, was keen to emphasise that Boyzone were still very much open for business. 'As long as our fans want to see us, it is safe to say we will stick around,' he said. 'We are all doing our own individual things as well. I've got a few things up my sleeve and I've just finished recording a couple of songs of my own.'

But, while his fellow band members were happily getting hitched, Stephen still had to maintain the fiction that he was looking for the right girl. He was now in his early twenties and, despite the numerous names that had been attached to him, it was well known that he had never had a girlfriend. Whether people suspected and didn't pry, or simply accepted the idea that he was looking for Miss Right, it's hard to say, but in the middle of 1998, when he was to all intents and purposes living with Eloy, there wasn't a word about it in the press.

Asked if he planned to get married any time soon, Stephen replied, 'The only woman in my life at the moment is my mum. She's like a best friend. I'm proud of her because she can do anything, from making the best dinners to chatting to our fans. She chats with the campers outside the house – they bring her chocolates and presents.'

What about Emma Bunton? 'Emma and I have the same sense of humour,' Stephen replied. 'And I think her voice is brilliant.' So, is there anyone else? 'Girls like All Saints are like us – they work hard. But they all have serious partners.' But did he feel like an outsider, given that the rest of the band was loved-up? 'Not at all! I'm happy the way I am and, if I'm meant to meet someone, I will.' Next, he was linked to Mandy Smith.

But his career was progressing, and, just as he said he wanted, Stephen was signed up to sing the soundtrack for the Disney film *Hercules*, as well as doing some work with Andrew Lloyd Webber. He was also, of course, settled in his personal life: he just couldn't talk about it yet.

Boyzone's next single, 'No Matter What', did well

too. Although the musical that it originated from didn't go down too well with the critics, the single went straight to No. 1, something with which Andrew Lloyd Webber publicly credited Stephen. 'It wouldn't have happened if Stephen Gately from Boyzone hadn't contacted Andrew two years ago to tell him how much he loved his musicals,' said a spokesman for Lloyd Webber. 'He actually went to Andrew's home and learned and performed the song.'

In turn, a rather excited Lloyd Webber joined the boys when they performed the song on *Top Of The Pops*.

Stephen then gave another interview about his search for love. 'I'm only 22 and I've been left on the shelf,' he said. 'I like a few drinks now and then, but I don't go mad. I like to feel fine in the morning, so I'm not too keen on getting hangovers. It's difficult finding the right type of woman. We're so busy and we're never in the same place that long to actually have a relationship with someone.'

But, er, three of the boys were now married and Mikey was engaged. 'The Boyzone family is getting bigger,' Stephen acknowledged. 'There's so many of us now but it's brilliant fun. I would like to be with someone, but the time's not right yet. If something happens, it happens, so I'm just gonna let things take their own course.'

Meanwhile, Ronan started to edge further away from the group; he and Louis began talks about managing another band together, just as Walsh had done with Boyzone. Indeed, Louis was bringing on a new boy band – Westlife. They were already being spoken of as the new Boyzone. Perhaps it really was time to move on.

The boys weren't just growing up and getting married: they were also beginning to become property owners. Stephen had made no secret of the fact that he wanted a big house and, while he was spending a lot of time in Holland with Eloy, he also invested in a converted mill in County Wicklow, something he was only too happy to show off. When in Dublin, he spent as much time with his family as possible – above all, with Michelle, who was by now married and had a two-year-old son, Jordan. Previously, Stephen had had a flat on the waterfront in Dublin, but this was his first big proper home.

Throughout his life, Stephen adored Disney, and Disney featured heavily in his new home. He displayed a copy of Disney's *The Art of Mulan* on his kitchen table and also owned a very rare copy of a Pocahontas doll given to him by a fan. Disney figurines were all over the house too. For a while, this was to be his refuge, although he would also start spending much more time in Holland, where Eloy was based.

He was becoming quite the collector. 'A lot of pop stars spend their money on wild living and cars – I prefer paintings and I drive a Peugeot 306,' he said. 'But I collect original Disney reproductions – I paid £9,000 for one recently; that's my biggest extravagance. I have a 1937 original sketch from *Snow White and the Seven Dwarfs* – my house is just like Disneyworld. I'm crazy about that stuff and that's my main addiction and obsession. I've got dozens of the things and they're worth thousands and thousands of pounds.'

He was proud of his pad and he couldn't stop talking about it. 'I've been lucky with the house and hope to have time to enjoy it in the future,' he said. 'I've got tons of people to thank for making it as wonderful as it is. My brother-in-law Alan Carr, who's an architect, discovered the building and redesigned it. It's taken him a whole year and he's done a fantastic job. My brother Mark, who's a carpenter, did all the woodwork and my friends, Orla Byrne and her boyfriend Greg, painted all the friezes and walls. I explained the Disney theme of the house and told them how I wanted it painted, then I let them do what they pleased.'

In retrospect, that interview was revealing in a very different way as well. Although it was to be a year before Stephen's rift with his family began, it is clear from reading between the lines that they were already growing apart. His life was now so far removed from what he had grown up with, that he and his parents didn't really understand one another any more.

'It's different with my mum and dad,' he admitted. 'It's not that they can't believe what I'm doing, it's more that they simply don't understand it. A lot of people who are very close to me don't understand. My mum and dad and brother Alan – who's two years older than me – don't get it. They just see all the glamour and all the hectic hard work behind the scenes.'

He was still, however, close to other members of his family. 'I generally talk to my sister Michelle, 24, brother Alan, 23, little brother Tony, 16, and my older brother Mark, 28,' he said. 'They all understand what I'm going through and they're very good to talk to. And my stylist, Alex, who's been on the road with Boyzone since we began five years ago, he's really good to talk to.'

Of course, where Stephen came from, it was practically unheard of to have a stylist: indeed, most people wouldn't have known such a thing existed. And so perhaps it wasn't surprising that he was growing away from his old friends, too. 'I don't really have many of the friends that I had before I was in the band,' he admitted. 'They just don't understand the lifestyle. But there are still a couple of best friends who are always there for me. When you come home and you catch up with everything in the first half an hour and you forget about work, things go back to how you used to be and you have a drink and a laugh.'

Of course, there was something else going on behind the scenes, too. Stephen was coming to terms not only with his fame, but also his homosexuality and it was that, as much as anything else, which was making him break from the past. But he was also discovering who he was, as all adults must do, and coming to terms with his new life. He liked to have friends round and cook for them, he said, and would relax by reading. Certainly, he had come a very long way since joining the band: 'I used to get homesick very badly,' he revealed. 'When I first went on tour when I was 17 years old, I would spend days in tears because I missed my parents' home so much. That went on for two years, but I carried on because it was a big opportunity. Now I love it – every time I go away, it's like a big adventure. I'm 22 years of age, and I've been to so many countries around the world – for free! How lucky can you get?'

And, despite constant reports that the band was to split, they soldiered on. Their personal lives continued to develop, too. Ronan's wife Yvonne discovered she was expecting their first child, while Mikey split from his girlfriend. Ronan's father Gerry was clearly suffering the loss of his wife as much as Ronan did: although his famous son had bought him a mansion, in the wake of Marie's death he could not bear to live in it any more and went off to a small rented flat.

Indeed, in some ways, there were strange parallels between Ronan and Stephen's lives, for Ronan was also not close to his father. 'There has always been a distance between me and my father,' he once said. 'My mam was everything to me, but my dad was never very emotional. He never showed us much love.'

More strangely still, before Ronan had got married, there were rumours that that much-vaunted virginity was actually a cover for something else – that *he* was gay. One interviewer put this to him, embarrassing him deeply, but what no one realised at the time, of course, was that, although Ronan wasn't gay, someone very close to him was. It was a question of right conclusion, wrong person – although Stephen certainly never made an issue about his own virginity.

The group had scored one of their biggest successes yet that year with the single 'No Matter What', and that was important in another way, in that the people who bought it were a little bit older than the band's traditional fans. If they were to have any longevity – and, despite the impending solo careers, the band never formally split – it was important to appeal to an older crowd, and they were managing it.

'I think it's simple – we've never lied or tried to fool the media and I like to think our music is constantly improving,' said Ronan. 'Also, we try to be decent and professional and that keeps people on our side. None of us ever dreamed Boyzone would still be going five years down the line, let alone still be having No. 1 albums. It's gone past all our expectations. We've sold more records in 1998 than ever before.

'"No Matter What" has been our biggest hit to date and "I Love The Way You Love Me" is doing really well. We've already started writing material for a new album and we're enjoying it too much to want to quit.'

More stories linking Stephen to eligible women appeared, although this was to be the last of them. Most of the other boys had settled down, and it was put about that Stephen was about to do likewise, with the Irish singer Kerri-Ann. She certainly knew the boys (which is more than can be said for some of the women that Stephen had been linked to), and, as usual, the exposure didn't do anyone's career any harm. Behind the scenes, though, everyone knew the truth now: Stephen was gay and it wasn't long before the rest of the world would know that, too.

By 1999, the boys were making plans for a greatest hits album, while their lifestyles continued to be far removed from where they had come from. Explaining his dietary regime, Stephen said, 'If we are out and about doing promotions and TV, it can be really hard to eat well. You just have to take what you can get at a service station. Sometimes, if I am conscious of having eaten really badly, I will have a day of eating just fruit and drinking water. On tour, I ask the caterers for healthy stuff – lots of chicken with pasta or rice and loads of fruit. I also make sure I have breakfast so I don't snack on chocolate too often. I am not very good at eating big plates of greens, though.'

It was a very long way from mashed potatoes with mince.

He was also watching himself now in a way that he had never done before. 'I would say my heath is not too bad,' he said. 'I am at my fittest when we are on tour because I do so much dancing. I'm also very careful with my diet – I can't afford to feel ill. You have to make sure you relax properly, otherwise touring can get very stressful and unhealthy. I am not really into huge parties, so I tend to take myself off to bed and have a good night's sleep. Sometimes I sleep till noon. I haven't been ill in over a year and hardly ever get bugs – I am very lucky in that way.'

And he was really sounding like a veteran of the show-business world when talking about his other habits, too. 'I used to drink a lot of beer, but I have cut back now,' he admitted. 'In the bar, after a show, I will have a few lagers – usually low-sugar – or sometimes a glass of orange juice. You have to make an effort in this business because there are always lots of smoky and boozy parties to avoid, if you want to keep fit.'

As the year went on, Ronan found himself in the interesting position of almost simultaneously becoming a father and having to deny that he'd had a gay affair – or, indeed, *any* affair. Rather, he was the doting father of baby Jack. But the fact that the rumours had surfaced at all meant that it was now only a matter of time before the band member who really was gay would be forced to speak out.

We will never know if Stephen would have openly declared his sexuality had he not been forced into it, but in the event he was enormously relieved to have done so. No longer would he have to put up with stories linking him to a series of women. Finally, he could admit to being who he truly was. But while there were plenty of singers out there who were openly gay, as a member of a boy band, Stephen found himself in a unique position: history was about to be made.

CHAPTER SIX

COMING OUT

The world of show business was awash with speculation. It had been an open secret in some circles for years now that a famous member of a boy band, frequently cited as a heartthrob to millions of teenage fans around the world, was, in fact, gay – but who was it? And would his secret ever come out?

Writing over a decade after Stephen Gately was forced to publicly declare his homosexuality, it is easy to forget just how much attitudes have changed since then. When George Michael first became a star, it would have been career suicide for him to openly admit he was gay, and he only did so years after his initial success with Wham! when, to all intents and purposes, it really didn't matter any more. The same applied to Sir Elton John, who was even married at one point to a German woman – Renate Blauel – before finding lasting happiness with David Furnish. Even as late as 1999, it was a hugely controversial and difficult decision that Stephen now had to take.

For years, he had been linked to women, including a former Miss Scotland called Isla Sutherland, Emma Bunton and the Irish singer Kerri-Ann – indeed, there had even been rumours of an engagement – whereas the reality, of course, was that he was living with Dutch boy-band singer Eloy de Jong. But, before his hand was forced in public, Stephen decided to tell his family the truth. They all took it well (and, after all, this was conservative Ireland, a Catholic country), starting, of course, with Michelle. She had known since 1995, a year after Stephen joined Boyzone. 'Steve, I always thought you were,' she simply replied.

Stephen then had to tell his father. 'I broke the news to my dad over a pint in our local pub in Dublin,' he revealed. 'I knew that, if my dad accepted the way I was, then my mum would. He just said, "Don't worry, son. We all love you."'

But now there was the matter of going public and that was no easy feat. For all that attitudes had changed hugely in the decades since homosexual acts had been decriminalised, the fact was that Stephen was still part of a band specifically designed to appeal to young women and there was concern that, by acknowledging he would never be interested in them, this might damage the brand. Ever since the early days of The Beatles, when John Lennon was forced to conceal the fact that he had a wife, a great deal of the marketing of such groups depended on an assumption of availability – and Stephen appeared to be the only one left. Ronan, Shane and Keith were all married, while Mikey was in a long-term relationship and had a child. If it came out that Stephen was gay, what would the news do to the band?

As a matter of fact, tensions, growing solo careers and a desire to branch out meant that the members of Boyzone were getting ready to call it a day anyway, but Stephen didn't know that then. Nor did anyone else. And so, in June 1999, it caused a sensation when Stephen became the first ever member of a boy band to publicly announce that he was gay.

His hand had been forced: a bodyguard was trying to sell the story. After an intensive discussion, a decision was made to do an interview with the *Sun*, a tabloid which had not always been gay-friendly in the past, in which he would come out. Under the strapline WORLD EXCLUSIVE came the headline: BOYZONE STEPHEN: I'M GAY AND I'M IN LOVE. Stephen was perfectly straightforward and told the world about

Eloy: 'I wanted my fans to hear the facts from me and Eloy before anyone got the chance to publish a twisted version of the truth,' he said. 'I hope the fans who have supported us from day one will respect my honesty.' And so they did.

Stephen further declared that he had known of his sexuality since he was 15. 'This is the hardest thing I have ever had to do, but I owe it to our fans – as well as to myself – to be completely honest,' he said. 'I know this may come as a bombshell to our followers. Many of them may be upset. I only hope they realise how important it is for me to reveal I am gay.'

He had known for weeks that this was on the cards. The roadie trying to sell the story had been hawking it round for some time now, and the news got back to Stephen. 'It was in Holland and I got a call from my press officer saying someone was trying to sell a story to the press,' he later recalled. 'I sat down and thought about it and I decided I'd rather someone didn't make any money from selling a story about me, I'd rather tell the fans myself. I think it's time.'

In the event, everyone was enormously supportive. Ronan, who was to provide such a heartfelt tribute at Stephen's funeral, immediately and publicly backed his friend. 'Stephen is one of my dearest friends in the world,' he said. 'Talking about this takes courage and I'll always love him for that.'

In fact, this certainly wasn't news to Boyzone, who had been well aware of the situation and were exceedingly sympathetic about it, too. 'The lads have always known and have always been cool about it, we've always had a laugh about it,' admitted Stephen, some months after the announcement. 'They've seen how difficult it's been for me on a day-to-day basis and they think, Good on ya. They've had girlfriends and gotten married, so they understand in a way. None of us ever had to hide. With me it was by choice, but they didn't hide their girlfriends or anything like that. We broke a lot of boundaries for boy bands – three of us have kids, some of us got married, all those things which don't normally happen. We broke all those barriers – you couldn't have a drink, you couldn't smoke. I don't think it could have worked for us with all those restrictions on us.'

They had also known from very early on. 'I just sat down with them and said, "You know, lads, there's something I've got to tell you," and they were really cool,' he continued. 'Very early on, about a couple of months after I joined the band, I think. They were just really cool, like I've said. We've always gotten on fantastically well. People just look and say, "I can't believe after all this time you can still laugh and joke, you can still stand each other," but we do – we're as close as brothers.'

And was he encouraged to hide it? 'No, no! They all left it to me. In fact, the lads encouraged me to come out earlier. They would say, "You know what, I think you should, and some time soon," and I said, "No, I'm not ready for it yet, I'm really not ready." They said it'd be a lot more relaxing for me. "You'll have your family, you'll have your fans, you'll have your friends and you'll have us. We'll stick by you, what more do you need?" I was nervous because I didn't know which way things would go, whether I would be accepted or whether I would be completely rejected by everyone.'

Back then, no one really knew how the news would be received. As for Stephen himself, he could only hope that this momentous step would not backfire. 'Stephen realises that the news will greatly shock many Boyzone fans, but he feels it's the best decision and hopes that they realise that people are different,' said a friend. 'He hopes that he and his boyfriend will be left alone and their privacy will be respected.'

In the event, the revelation did not do him any harm in the slightest – in fact, almost everyone seemed to realise immediately just quite what a difficult step this had been and to praise Stephen for it. Nor did industry insiders think that he had done himself, or the band, any harm. John McKie, editor of *Smash Hits* at the time, observed, 'Ronan got married, losing his single status, and went on to win three *Smash Hits* awards this year. I think Stephen will still be immensely popular. No one's ever come out at the height of their career before. It's very brave and honest of Stephen. I think the fans will be very supportive.'

Gennaro Castaldo, of the HMV record chain, agreed. 'Now this is out in the open, he can relax,' he said. 'The coverage of the story has come across in a very empathetic way and the high profile it has been given can only help sales.'

Unsurprisingly, though, there were also some negative ramifications, one of which cast a shadow over Stephen's relationship with his mother that would go on for years. First, however, Stephen and Eloy had to put up with Eloy's previous lover, a Dutch television presenter called Carlo Boszhard, telling his story – something that would have been unthinkable only weeks previously.

Carlo and Eloy had been together for five years, living in the village of Nieuwendam, outside Amsterdam. 'I still love Eloy and I think it is a shame that we are no longer together and won't grow old together as we once hoped,' Carlo said. 'I had always hoped we would kiss and make up because we have unfinished business together and a special love. But, when Eloy told me two weeks ago he was in love with Steve, I finally realised there was no chance.'

It had all been a little complicated. Stephen and Eloy actually met in 1995, but didn't become close until November 1998. The relationship between Eloy and his former lover was rocky, with an initial break after Eloy's band, Caught In The Act, went off on tour. 'I told him I couldn't live with that any longer,' said Carlo. 'We had a long and emotional talk, during which we both cried. I decided we didn't have a future any more. We stayed best of friends, but we couldn't revive our love. To be honest, even up until a couple of weeks ago, I hoped we'd start all over again, but when he told me about Stephen and their affair, I knew there was no chance any more.'

Eloy did, however, warn Carlo that he and Stephen were about to go public, something which shocked him to the core. 'I was very, very surprised, to say the least, given the fact that he'd been so reluctant to reveal his love for me for so long,' he said. 'I found it hard to understand how he could love Stephen, because I thought, after being with me, he would rather have an unknown boyfriend, with whom he could live anonymously.

'I suppose, even though I caused the first rift, Eloy has ended up breaking my heart. I just hope he is truly happy with Stephen and doesn't end up breaking his heart, too. I have met Steve many times, even when I was with Eloy, but never could I have expected he would be my lover's new love. I didn't even know he was gay. I haven't spoken to Steve since, but I spoke to Eloy today. I think it is brave what they are doing because the whole world is watching, especially because Eloy is starting a new career as a TV presenter in Germany.

'Eloy was a star on his own, but from now on he will be seen as the gay lover of Steve from Boyzone. I wonder if that's easy to live with. I had to leave his home in the early hours to prevent fans seeing me. I had more and more troubles with that because I felt I was lying to the public and eventually I came out as gay. That felt very good.'

Stephen was well and truly out now too, and with a huge weight off his mind. Speaking again to the *Sun*, he said, 'There were thousands of faxes and emails. It's great that the fans are behind me and I can now carry on with my pop career.'

That much was certainly true: it was very quickly becoming apparent that the revelations had done no damage at all to his career. But revelations continued to pour in from people who might have remained quiet in the past: this time around about a previous lover, Stephen Howard, who committed suicide at the age of 21. He had become a heroin addict and then turned to crime.

Stephen Howard's mother Bernie now spoke out. 'I can't say that the break-up was the reason for my Stephen getting into drugs, but there was no sign of any problem before that,' she said sadly. 'Stephen Gately was a lovely boy, and I was very, very fond of him. He and my Stephen were like two peas in a pod, they did everything together. It never crossed my mind that they were lovers in a sexual way at the time, but it became obvious later that they were. I wasn't surprised when Stephen Gately issued his statement saying that he was gay. I think that everyone who knew him had realised that a long time ago and it didn't bother anyone in the least.'

What made it particularly sad was that Stephen Howard had had his own show-business ambitions, too. But, as his ex-lover's career took off into the stratosphere, the former young hopeful's life went into sharp decline. 'The two lads were the best of pals,' continued Bernie. 'They used to practise dance routines together and went in for talent contests all over the place. Not long after Stephen Gately got picked for Boyzone, the two of them split up. Boyzone had a squeaky-clean image right from the start. The lads were controlled every minute of the day and Louis Walsh, their manager, wanted them to make a clean break away from their past.

'Even at their very earliest shows, when they were just starting to hit the big time, he was trying to run their lives. He dictated what they ate, what they wore, where they went and who they talked to – anybody from their past who might prove embarrassing in the future was ruled out completely. If they handed out tickets to their old friends from north Dublin, he would get very angry and he didn't like it if he saw the boys talking to their old mates afterwards.'

Of course, what Louis was doing was building the boys into massive stars and, if that meant protecting their image as much as he was able to, then so be it. But, as Stephen Gately began to grow away from his old life and build up a new one, poor Bernie had to watch her own son moving in a very different direction.

'He started taking ecstasy at raves and then moved on to heroin,' she revealed. 'Like a lot of other mothers, I never realised that he was taking drugs until it was too late. Looking back, it is easy to see the signs, but you just don't ever think it is going to come knocking on your door, too. Stephen Gately did his best to help my Stephen, but there was very little that he could do. He talked to him and tried to persuade him that he was going to kill himself with the drugs, but I think my son was just too far gone by that stage. I don't blame Stephen Gately in the least. I'm still very fond of him and glad he has done so well for himself. But there he is, rich and famous, while my Stephen is four years in his grave.'

It was a sorry tale and a testament to the sweetness of Stephen's character that his ex-lover's mother still bore him such goodwill, despite the tragic fate of her own son. But what was to prove far more serious to him in the longer term was his own mother Margaret's reaction to the revelations. Stephen was giving every sign of being hugely relieved that his sexuality was now out in the open, but Margaret was adamant that he was unhappy. Worse still, given that Stephen had come out via the pages of the *Sun* newspaper, his mother chose the *Mirror*, deadly rival to the *Sun*, to launch what almost appeared to be a counterattack.

'Stephen wasn't ashamed of his sexuality, but he never wanted people to know about it,' she said. 'Because it was always his own business and that is the way it should be. I think what has happened is blackmail. I always thought my children should never be pressurised, but Stephen has been bullied into doing this.'

Indeed, Margaret went further still, saying the announcement would have a damaging effect. 'We have been going through hell since we were told that this was going to be published,' she said. 'I haven't slept for a week. The effect it will have on the whole family will be phenomenal; everyone has been so worried. I have problems with my lungs and I'm afraid that the stress of this will affect my illness. All of us are involved in this. I have to go out and do my day's work with the whole place looking at me.'

In many ways, this was understandable: Margaret was indeed about to find herself at the centre of intensive speculation. But, not having the horde of media advisers around her that were on hand to look after Boyzone, she couldn't have realised that she was putting a negative impact on a story that had actually been brushed with a remarkably positive slant. She was taking the allegations personally, whereas they were about Stephen and not her, and she was also undermining his stance that there was nothing to be ashamed of and that a great weight had now been lifted from him. And Stephen was absolutely livid. A rift formed between mother and son that only healed shortly before his death.

Stephen himself was adamant that it was entirely his own decision. He also spoke very warmly about the newspaper in which he came out. 'At the end of the day, nobody forced me, it was my decision,' he said. 'Things could have come out at any time and people could have said whatever they wanted, but I wanted people to hear what I had to say. And at the end of the day, everything was done the way I wanted it to be done, let's put it like that. And I wasn't forced at all, absolutely not. The *Sun* have been great, they've really helped me – actually, all the papers. We have a very young audience and they were very sympathetic towards all of the different audiences.'

And he continued to emphasise that it had not been easy – far from it: 'At the time when I decided to do the story, I remember suddenly feeling that I wanted to cry. You know, I was scared. And then I thought, Well, I can either break down and cry, or stand up and be strong about things, and that's what I tried to do. It's my life and you've only got one – you could be knocked down by a bus tomorrow. You should just get on with your life and try and do the best you can.'

And although Stephen's circumstances were unusual – indeed, unprecedented at the time when he came out – he was keen to emphasise that it could be an extremely difficult move to make, whatever your profession. 'It's very difficult whether you're a doctor, a nurse, a student, whoever you are,' he said. 'It can still be a real issue, even though it shouldn't be.

'Late at night, the night before the story broke, sitting in the bedroom in a hotel, myself and Eloy were watching *Sky News* and they said, "Let's have a look at tomorrow's papers" and there I was on four front pages, which was, erm, quite a shock. I'm just a normal lad from Dublin. Why is this going on all over the world? It was even in the *New York Post*! There are wars, people dying and horrific things happening all over the world, why not try and make that better, have a look at those issues? There are more important things than someone's sexuality.'

But the deed had finally been done and Stephen was beginning to sound relaxed in a way that he had never really done before. 'I used to be paranoid about what people thought of me – upset, depressed,' he said in an interview that he and Michelle gave jointly in the *Sunday Times*. 'I just wanted to close the door behind me and stay in all the time. I was closed and unhappy and not right in myself. I felt, I can't deal with this. Maybe because I felt I couldn't be totally myself.

'I desperately wanted to be a pop star, but decided early on I couldn't do that and be gay. I had to keep it to myself – being honest would mean saying goodbye to fame. I was so desperate to succeed and thought that, if suppressing my feelings was the way to do it, then so be it.'

But, of course, it had just made him unhappy, not least because he was constantly on edge with worry that someone would spill the beans. 'I was the only one in the band that didn't have a girlfriend or wife,' he continued. 'Journalists often asked me if I was seeing anyone and I always managed to evade the issue without telling a lie. But the whole thing gave me sleepless nights. When I found out that someone was trying to sell the story that I was gay, I decided I wanted the fans to hear it from me. And now the lads are saying, "We've never seen you happier in all the six years we've been together."'

This message was reinforced courtesy of another interview that Stephen did shortly after he came out. Far from causing the problems that his mother had fretted about, for the first time since he became famous, he could now live openly with Eloy without worrying what would happen if anyone saw them together.

'Life just couldn't be better for me,' he said. 'I can do whatever I want, now. Things like going to the cinema and eating out are as normal for us as any other couple. I always worried that someone would take a picture of me with Eloy because not everybody knew I was gay. Now we do whatever we want and I can get on with my life, with being Stephen Gately. We can go on the same flight when we go on holiday and even go to the duty-free shop together. It was a nightmare before, having to get separate flights to wherever we went. All the pressures have gone, it's a wonderful feeling.'

Of course, the reaction he received had had a huge amount to do with it. So many people had been supportive and it was so obvious that there would be no adverse effect on his career that all those previous concerns just drifted away. 'I love reading the fans' letters – they really cheer me up,' Stephen confided. 'Some days I feel a bit down, but I cheer myself up by reading a few of the letters. It's been absolutely overwhelming and I know I've done the right thing. After I've finished, I always feel full of life and get all this energy – it's wonderful.'

But it had been an extraordinary experience, as he himself admitted. Because no one in his position had ever done this before, there was no clue as to what would happen next. 'I was absolutely terrified the night before the story was about to break,' Stephen recalled. 'I remember sitting in a hotel in Amsterdam, having a drink and hoping all my fans would support me; it was very worrying because they could have gone either way – I was so nervous.

'The next morning when I woke up, I put the TV on and it was everywhere. It was really weird. That was an experience I will remember for the rest of my life. I was so happy and relieved that all the fans were very supportive of my decision. I received boxes and boxes of letters and presents; I just couldn't be happier. Eloy and I are just getting on with things.'

Now that he could finally talk about it, he scarcely seemed able to hold anything back. 'It was really difficult for a couple of years, and it's difficult when every night you go to bed thinking, Shit, what's going to be in the paper the next day, will they find out?' he told another magazine. 'Magazines always asked me about settling down and I would say, "When I meet the right person and fall in love." I never said when I meet the right girl because I didn't want to blatantly lie – I tried to be an honest person. There was a lot of pressure when the guys were all getting girlfriends and they'd say, "You're the only member left, what's happened?"'

But it had not been easy. 'It was very, very frightening, but I try not to look back at that,' he said. 'I just feel sorry for anybody else within the business who is gay and feels trapped – it can be really awful, worrying all the time, and people might not handle it as well as I did.'

But support really had flooded in from all quarters, and some very famous ones at that. Other celebrities who had had to come out were, for obvious reasons, enormously supportive, something Stephen could scarcely believe to be the case. 'I got letters from all different walks of life – mums, dads, children, male, female,' he recalled. 'I got a big book with over 1,000 messages from people left on the Internet, phone calls from everybody: George Michael phoned my manager's office, I got flowers from Elton John and David, Lily Savage; Graham Norton wrote me a letter and it all meant so much to me. Hopefully, it won't hurt my career that much. Maybe I'll even gain some fans.

'People had been kind in their letters as well, saying, "You've done a lot for gay people and for teenagers or adults who want to come out," and that's the really touching thing – that out of something so controversial can come some good,' he continued. 'I've had all the letters shipped out to Holland, and every morning when I get up, I read two or three of them and I'm going to get through all of them.'

And, at the end of the day, what had all the fuss really been about? Stephen was, as he said himself, a perfectly normal man in a perfectly normal relationship – it was just that it happened to be with someone of the same sex. He talked about the life he had with Eloy, sounding just like an old married couple: 'We don't go out to clubs – I hate clubs, I never go dancing. We tend to do things like go to the movies or watch a video at home. Like last night, we stayed in with a bottle of wine and watched *Patch Adams*. We walk our dog together – a little Schitzhu called Joey – and just do everyday things. We're not into going out and coming in at two or three in the morning. I'd rather go out early for a meal, have a glass of wine and come home.

'I'm not a majorly nineties person – I'm a bit old-fashioned when it comes to things like that, but that's just me, I enjoy it. Plus, this lifestyle is so busy – you're constantly doing interviews or flying around, or rehearsing. I have a day off tomorrow, so I'll probably get up, chuck on a tracksuit and a coat, and we'll drive down to the beach and take Joey for a walk, have some lunch and do simple, nice little things. Any time that we have together, we make the most of – we're never, ever apart anywhere that I go, unless it's work. We're very, very happy together and it's great: it's everything I've always wanted.'

And now he could be totally open about it all, too. Stephen was so happy that he was talking about adopting, perhaps, and all the happiest elements of life that most people look for, whether they are gay, straight or somewhere in the middle. Life would never be the same, but it would be an awful lot simpler from then on.

But for all that he played down what he'd done, saying that he was just a normal bloke, Stephen had carved out his own little chunk of history. Until now, a man in his position who had been marketed to appeal to girls would indeed have been extremely vulnerable to issues such as blackmail and all the concomitant mental stress that involved. From then on, things changed. Stephen Gately had come out as gay, the world continued to rotate on its axis and no one batted an eyelid. What exactly was the big deal?

And from that moment on, it became easier for stars to be open about their sexual orientation – when Will Young came out a couple of years later, there was no shame and no subsequent loss of popularity. Stephen Gately was gay – so what?

CHAPTER SEVEN

GOING IT ALONE

As the repercussions of what was then deemed to be a sensational disclosure began to die down, there were to be some very fundamental shifts in Stephen's life, which would completely change the way he had been going about things for years. On the most obvious and fundamental level, he was now free of pretence, could live openly with Eloy and show the world the person he really was. That was a phenomenal relief. But, at the same time, it was beginning to seem that his parents, especially his mother, were nothing like as accepting of the situation as they first appeared. Towards the end of Stephen's life, they would completely change their view, but, at the time, it seems they found having an openly gay and very famous son too much to deal with. The formerly close family began to split apart.

It was a situation Eloy understood, and it wasn't just Stephen who had openly come out – of course, Eloy had done so too. He was a big star in mainland Europe and the story made the front pages, especially in Germany. And he had had a difficult time telling his parents, too. 'I was 17 when I went to my sister Lucienne to tell her the truth,' he revealed. 'On the same evening, I went to my mum and said, "I have to talk to you. What do you think, do you think I love girls or boys?" and she said, "I think you love boys." She was great and really understood and helped me.

'But it took a year until she told it to my father. He was beside himself with rage and didn't want to have anything to do with me any more from that moment on. One year, he didn't talk a word to me. He despised me and made me feel that everything I touched was dirty then. These have been the most awful years in my life!'

And they were never reconciled. Eloy's father had died some years previously, never having accepted the truth about his son. 'The relationship between my father and me has never been very good – unfortunately,' Eloy admitted. 'When I got famous with Caught In The Act, he said he would accept my feelings, but he never really did. He said to me again and again, "The most beautiful girls are crazy for you. I don't understand why you don't have sex with them." Today, I really wished he could see how happy I am with Stephen!'

It was quite a change from the way Stephen had been living before.

Nor was everything as it had been within Boyzone. In early 2000, they had been together for the best part of six years – more, if you count the early days before they made it – and everyone, with the possible exception of Shane, was keen to try something new.

Ronan, Stephen and Mikey were all thinking about solo singing careers, Keith was considering television and Shane talked about driving rally cars. There were no plans to break Boyzone up per se, but everyone seemed to be wanting a bit of a break.

Ever the pragmatist, Ronan was looking to the longer term and his thoughts about the future were to prove absolutely correct. 'Obviously things can never be the same again,' he said. 'Even if we come back together for an event, we'll be different people. But it would be a shame to let it wither. We'd be very lucky if all five of us are successful at what we want to do as individuals; I don't think that will happen. What it will come down to is who works the hardest.'

And he certainly intended to work his socks off: in other interviews, he'd spoken of his fear of meeting the same fate as Gary Barlow. Gary is now, of course, an international star again, but, in the immediate aftermath of the break-up of Take That, his career sank without a trace, while Robbie Williams, totally unexpectedly, went global. Ronan was keen to avoid that same fate.

Besides, the rest of the band agreed with him. 'It wouldn't make business sense to split forever,' admitted Mikey. 'There's no point cutting off our nose to spite our face. Boyzone was something we all enjoyed, but it was a job too, and we were always men enough to know, with families and responsibilities, that, if any of us had a problem with someone else in the band, we had to sort it out and get on with the job.'

Shane was feeling slightly annoyed with Louis, who had other fish to fry, not least the up-and-coming Westlife. 'We've grown up in each other's pockets and we need a break, to find ourselves again and come back stronger than ever,' he said. 'Louis was saying a lot of things he shouldn't be saying. He may have his ideas about Westlife coming along and killing Boyzone, but that's not how we think. Louis Walsh has no authority to speak on Boyzone's behalf – he doesn't know what's going on.'

That was a little harsh, although Louis undoubtedly had other interests to pursue. 'They have had five great years,' he said. 'They don't want to flog a dead horse or become Status Quo. There's talk of doing a summer tour, but to do that they'll need a new record out and there's nothing in the schedule. It's now up to Stephen and Ronan, if they want to neglect their solo careers and get back with the band to tour.'

Certainly, it was a new opportunity for Stephen. He was to release his first solo single, the aptly titled 'A New Beginning', in May. This would not only be a solo venture, but also a way of judging how fans would react to his new status. He was quietly confident. 'My fans have been absolutely brilliant,' he said. 'I don't think that because I'm gay people won't go out and buy my new single. My new song is about making a new beginning, being true to who I really am. I want people to listen to my music, not worry about my sexuality.'

The launch was held in London – all the Boyzone members were there, apart from Mikey. There was a pretty good celebrity turnout: Dale Winton, Alan Davies and Rajesh Mirchandani, among others, with a very nervous Stephen. 'I am nervous and excited,' he admitted. 'The most nerve-wracking time for me will be the day the single is released. It feels weird doing all this without the rest of the band after everything I've been through with them.'

Mikey was also putting out a single – 'You're My Angel' inspired by his daughter Hanna. 'Hanna's the angel in my life, and, when some things were going wrong, she was the one that was there for me with her unconditional love and innocence,' he revealed. 'However, it's a general song. It's just about the special somebody in everyone's life.

'My sister Catherine is a singer, too. She flew in from New York to help me out and did the backing vocals. I suppose you could say that musical talent runs in the family. When we were growing up, there was always someone singing somewhere. I've always written my own material, so it's very exciting to be playing on my own now. I've been so used to having four other people around me it becomes security after a while. So I feel quite exposed and it will take me a bit of time to adjust.'

Inevitably, rumours of rivalries between the boys began to emerge. It couldn't have been otherwise: given the immediate example of what can happen when a boy band splits, as experienced by Take That, and also given the fact that they all seemed to be putting out singles at pretty much the same time, there was bound to be speculation that each one wanted to win the competition to do well alone.

Mikey, however, denied any straightforward competition with Stephen, fuelled by the fact that he hadn't turned up to his band mate's launch. 'There was no truth in the rumour that I had deliberately stayed away from Stephen's launch or that we had fallen out,' he stated. 'Our singles are totally different musically, anyway. There's no way we are in competition with one another. Had I known about the launch, I would have been the first one there to support Stephen. There are some people who want to poison things and drive a wedge between us to create hype, but we are too good friends to ever let that happen.'

Indeed, as with so many members of now disbanded boy bands, Mikey suddenly felt free to shake off the shackles and reveal the reality behind the squeaky-clean Boyzone image. 'The reason we kept up our clean-cut image was not because we were clean-cut guys,' he admitted. 'We all had a drink, one of us is gay, and I smoked 40 cigarettes a day until I gave up two and a half months ago. We knew we had a young audience, who would be easily influenced, and we didn't want to promote drinking or smoking to children – that's why we kept it clean in public. But, as soon as we were on our own, we went straight to the bar.'

Then there were the drugs. 'I never took ecstasy or cocaine or heroin, or anything like that,' Mikey continued. 'I'd be worried I'd be the one in a million it would kill – or else that I'd like it too bloody much and wouldn't want to stop. The only thing I've ever done is smoke a joint, but it's not a way of life, just something I'd do once in a while with my mates for a giggle.

'Like most Irish families growing up, alcohol problems were always around us and I do think drink is the worst of all evils. Compare that with somebody having a joint – it's the complete opposite. They are not going to have the energy to rob a car; it will be all laughs and giggles and going for something to eat. I believe cannabis should be legalised for medicinal purposes. If it relieves pain, how can we deny that relief to people who suffer?'

And then there was Stephen. 'He was only 16 at the start and it was a very difficult time for him,' he said. 'The poor guy went to hell and back. When he felt ready and strong enough to come out, he did it. It was a very brave thing for him to do and he had the support of everyone around him.'

In the event, it was Mikey's comments about drugs, not Stephen, that went on to cause a row (Stephen himself was bedridden with a painful case of kidney stones). Indeed, the Parents Council of Ireland, along with various politicians came down very heavily on Mikey, forcing him to speak out again. 'I want to tell people that I didn't mean to cause an outrage,' he said. 'I'm devastated about the image that has been portrayed of me. Yes, I said that I think cannabis should be legalised, but for medical purposes.

'Other newspapers made me out to be a rogue. Because of how they have twisted it, people could think I'm some kind of mad drug-taking pop star and I want to assure them that I am not. They've jumped to the wrong conclusions. I said what I said not to cause outrage, but to put a point of view across.

'Yes, I smoked pot sometimes, but so have a lot of people. I don't want that to be a reason for young people to go out and start taking drugs; that was the last thing on my mind. I am a dad myself, and I would never want my child to take drugs, but I still say that I don't think cannabis is as big a scourge on society as alcohol. I feel that I've been stitched up by some of the downmarket tabloids.'

It was interesting that of the two big admissions, Stephen's about being gay and Mikey's about taking drugs, it was the second and not the first that caused a really big fuss.

Stephen himself was now concentrating on launching his solo career. This was the perfect opportunity to carve out a new niche for himself. 'I want to steer away from my image as the cute little one,' he said. 'I was a teenager when I started and now I'm 24. I think people will be surprised at how different my own music is to what I do in Boyzone. In the band I have always done the high notes, but fans will see another side of me.

139

'I wanted to get away from the ballad-type songs people associate with me. The album has a real dance beat because I love disco music and I love dancing. The first single has lots of energy. I've worked extremely hard on this album, but I'll be hiding at home when it's released, praying that people will like it. If it goes well, I will do a solo tour.'

Of course, in many ways, this was a return to how he started – as a disco dancer, not a balladeer.

Ronan was constantly worried about the possibility of burnout; so too was Stephen. 'It got to the point when I needed to do something about my health and lifestyle, otherwise I would have collapsed,' he admitted. 'I told our manager I needed a couple of days off, every couple of weeks. I also went to a lady for acupuncture, which was amazing. After a few sessions, I suddenly started to laugh and feel full of energy. I meditate, which helps enormously, and I've been taught relaxation techniques, which I now practise at home. I only go back for treatment now and again to get me back on track, but it's been a transformation.'

He was also so much happier now that he could openly spend time with Eloy in the house, just outside Amsterdam. 'It's beautiful and calm there and I go over to see Eloy as much as I can,' he said. 'We're very committed, we get on so well. My sister and her husband brought my nephew Jordan, and my brother

Mark and his wife brought their son over for the Millennium celebrations and we all had a wonderful time. In Ireland, I have a motor boat and I love spending money on clothes, but I'm not foolish with it and I will always remember where I came from.'

As the launch of the single approached, however, Stephen's health problems worsened. This was not a good omen: he was forced to have an operation to deal with the kidney stones, but it was scheduled just as the single was due to come out. Given the kind of publicity necessary to launch a new record by then, this was causing serious problems.

'It's very stressful for Stephen,' said a friend close to him. 'He's had to miss out on all sorts of promotional work and TV appearances that would have gone with the single. Even so, he'll just be happy when the op is done and he's feeling 100 per cent again.'

In the event, the single entered the charts at No. 3.

Something else that was on the cards was working with Eloy, although Stephen was a little more circumspect about that. 'Everybody's been asking if we'll do a duet,' he said. 'I'd like to work together with him, writing for his album or something, but I can't imagine a duet.'

He really was revelling in his newfound freedom: he was enjoying talking about his life with Eloy and announced that they were even thinking of adopting children. 'I wouldn't give them a name that would get them kicked around in the school playground,' he said happily. 'Eventually, I would love a kid. And, as I've made a bit of money, I'd put them through a good school. I know what it's like to struggle as I came from a really poor background.'

But, just for now, he was concentrating on his musical career. 'It's one of the happiest times of my life,' he said. 'I'm very fortunate to be in the position that I am in at the moment. I'm about to venture out with a solo album, and I'm in a very good relationship. I've got two dogs and a lovely house in Ireland – the dogs are called Joey and Woody. Eloy got me Woody for my birthday. He's a Meron cocker spaniel and is dead cute.'

But, like any couple, the two argued occasionally. 'Just very little, silly things – the same as anyone else,' Stephen said. 'We argue over a fork or a table, or something – stuff like that – ridiculous things, really. We spend a lot of time together at home. I love my house – I hardly ever go out clubbing. I like to sit down and socialise, have dinner or a couple of beers and a chat, rather than going out and dancing.'

And because he was spending so much time in Holland, he decided to sell the house in Ireland, putting it on the market for £475,000. And as Stephen was now very comfortable with being out,

Louis also felt able to admit that, had he known the big secret at the time of his audition, his protégé would probably not have got the gig.

'I did not know Stephen was gay when we gave him the job in Boyzone,' he stated. 'I think I would have thought twice about it at the time. I wouldn't now, but definitely back then I would have because it wasn't cool at the time.'

Rather ironically, everything considered, Louis found himself on the receiving end of a counterblast for his remarks. He was only being honest – after all, boy-band members are supposed to appeal to girls – but the renegade cleric Pat Buckley, who a few months previously had come out as being gay himself, took it amiss. 'What he said was totally homophobic,' he protested. 'I think it's a criminal offence in Ireland to say something homophobic like that. He's a very stupid man to say such a stupid thing. I would have thought that there were enough gay and bi-sexual people in the pop industry for it to be totally normal. He [Stephen] was very brave to come out and I admired it at the time. I was thinking of doing it for a few years and it was good to see some Irish people who were prepared to nail their colours to the mast.'

Louis himself recalled how everyone tried to keep the truth about Stephen a secret until he was ready to come out. 'I don't think he could have done it three years ago,' he admitted. 'We hid it for a long, long time. It was absolutely nerve-wracking for Stephen. He told me he dreaded the story coming out and so did I, because I thought it would affect his fan base. But we did not get one bad phone call or letter about it.'

In fact, at this point Louis was keen to set the record straight about a number of things, including the truth about what happened with Richie Rock. 'I had given Richard two or three chances,' he revealed. 'I thought he would be like his father and be very professional, but let's just say he was unprofessional and that is why I had to chop him.

'At the original audition we only got 150 people and we picked the best of what we got. It was an attitude more than anything. Boy bands work much harder than rock bands – it's all promotion, you are constantly out there promoting yourself. You have to be totally dedicated; it's like a football team. If somebody is not right in the team, there is always somebody waiting to take their place.'

As to the future, Louis was managing Ronan, but he was also thinking about another possibility: a duet between Keith and Shane. This was also quite a step further in other ways, for, in a rather unkind moment, Louis once described them as 'excess baggage'.

'I am making a record with Shane and Keith next

week,' he announced. 'It is a Milli Vanilli song. We are taking the piss out of ourselves, but they are singing on the track and it is going to be a huge hit.'

But of Boyzone itself, Louis believed – wrongly, as things would turn out – that it really was all over now. 'I think they are finished,' he said. 'They all have solo careers. I only manage Ronan now; he is a fantastic worker. The world always needs another boy band, every generation wants their own boy band – you can get five years out of them.'

In fact, Boyzone had had more than five years, but, clearly, Louis was now focused elsewhere.

Stephen's home life was so contented that he was seriously beginning to think about adoption, a preoccupation that would stay with him until the end of his life. At this time, in the middle of 2000, there had been much in the news about Tony Barlow and Barrie Drewitt, two gay men who caused uproar when they fathered surrogate twins in the US and then brought them back to the UK to bring them up as a family unit. Coming out was one thing, but a gay couple bringing up children was still seen in some circles to be a step too far. Nonetheless, Stephen was adamant this was what he wanted to do.

'I've always wanted kids, ever since I could remember,' he said. 'I've got a lot of security to offer a child and you shouldn't leave it too late to have one.

Ronan had his first one at 22. I'm 24 now, so it's not too early. I'd make sure he or she was comfortable, but also that they respected what they had and were aware that some people have very little money. To me, though, the most important lesson in life a child can learn is to have manners. I hate rudeness and people being judgemental – it costs nothing to be nice and manners go a long way in life.'

But what of the furore surrounding Barlow and Drewitt? Stephen didn't seem unduly concerned. 'Yes, I do know about the gay dads,' he admitted. 'I've read the news about them and think, Good on them! And I don't really know where we stand in this country on gay couples adopting children. Eloy and I still have to look into all of this.

'All I know is I'm good with babies. I've always loved them and I love being with children. I used to teach them drama and dance years ago. My four-year-old nephew Jordan is also my godson. He's a good kid and has been good training for me. His mother, my sister Michelle, is expecting her second child in November – I can't wait.'

One reason why Stephen was so set on this course was because, back then, it seemed that he and Eloy would be together for good. 'I've found the love of my life, he's really sweet, very sensitive, handsome, tall and he's my best friend,' he revealed. 'I once even sent him 500 white roses with one red rose in the middle when I was going away for a few days. We're like two lads together, really. We go to the pub and have a drink, play darts, pool and video games. We do our weekly grocery shopping together. In fact, we do everything together.'

And he was keen to emphasise that Eloy was just as big a name as he himself was. 'Yeah, he's a big star on the Continent,' he said. 'The Backstreet Boys even supported his band, which shows how massive they are. He really understands what I've gone through. I've met his family and he's met mine. They all get on great and his family are lovely: his mum looks after our dogs, Joey and Woody, when we're away from Holland. I've also learned a bit of Dutch but it's nothing like Eloy, who is fluent in three different languages.'

Stephen was now preparing for the release of his second single, 'I Believe', which was on the soundtrack of *Billy Elliot* and which, as a ballad, was rather closer to the types of songs that he had previously been associated with. 'A lot of solo artists make the mistake of doing something very different to what they're known for,' he said, backtracking rather on what he had stated when his first single was released. 'With this, and especially with the first single, everyone expected a ballad. It's a lot harder to crack the charts with an up-tempo song. If some people want to say it's very similar to Boyzone, then I take that as a big compliment.'

His involvement with the film and, indeed, his wish to make plans for the future was making him think about the possibilities of appearing on the big screen. As a young boy, he had acted and enjoyed the experience, so why not make a return? 'I really want to get into acting,' he told one interviewer. 'I'd love to play a really bad villain, or a comedy Goody Two-Shoes. I couldn't be an action hero because I'm too small, but I'd love to be in the next Guy Ritchie movie.

'I wouldn't do love scenes with women. And I won't get naked – unless they paid me a shitload of money! The same goes with going full-frontal in a magazine. I'd do it, but for nothing less than a million! No one's asked me yet. I mean, who'd wanna see me nude?'

Stephen was joking, of course, but was simply so content now that he could poke fun at himself. 'Some papers said I've been spending so much time in Amsterdam because we plan to get married there,' he continued. 'But gay couples can get married in lots of places these days – Amsterdam, Las Vegas, even in England – so it doesn't necessarily have to be in Holland.

'As for the adoption rumours, we haven't looked into it seriously. But I adore kids – I'd love to give a kid a chance. I come from an underprivileged background, so wouldn't think twice about adopting a Kosovan baby, or another child affected by war. [But] I never babysit for Ronan Keating! He's never asked me! I'd take Jack to the pub and sneak a whiskey in the bottle!'

And there were other ways of going about having children, too. 'Anything's possible these days,' said Stephen. 'On Oprah Winfrey the other day there was a man who had biological twins by two separate women after splitting the egg. So, in theory Eloy and I could impregnate the same woman with each of our sperm and have one twin that was mine, and one that was his. It's mad, isn't it?'

Despite his newfound openness and contentment, however, Stephen retained the nervous streak that he'd had since childhood, although he was now able to talk about it more. 'When Eloy's not there, I sleep with the light on because I'm scared of spirits,' he said. 'I saw a woman in a hotel room I stayed in, and a couple of years earlier – in the same hotel in London – I awoke hearing this scratching. I told the manager, and he said that a couple had a row in the room and the man locked his partner in a chest and she suffocated. That was the scratching!'

Keith was certainly able to back that one up. 'He's a very spiritual person,' he said. 'He has some form of sixth sense and sees spirits everywhere. He would get very frightened in a hotel room on his own. I would ask, "Do you want to come over?" And he would say, "Yes, will you come and get me?"

'I would have to put on my robe and go and pick him up, and he would sleep in my room. I am not the least bit homophobic and, if it made him feel comfortable, then fine. Stephen has had a tough old life. I knew he was gay from the start, though he kept denying it to us for a while. After he told the band, it was a long time before the press found out. Now he's the most friendly, open and honest guy. He is so in love.'

But, as Stephen sought to make a success of his solo career, there was a hint of ructions to come. His first single had got to a perfectly respectable No. 3, but he (and the other boys) were being trounced by Ronan, whose solo career would soon far outpace that of his old band. His latest single, 'Life Is A Rollercoaster', was at No. 1; four of the five solo albums he made by the time of Stephen's death also hit the top slot.

It was to lead, in the short term, to a rift – none of the other boys, not even Stephen, the *de facto* number two in Boyzone, could compete with that. But Ronan was still standing up for his band mates. And, as for the ongoing debate about whether Stephen and Eloy should be able to adopt, he was very much with them on this: 'I do know from having a child that it's very important for a child to be with its mother,' he said. 'But I know Stephen and I know Eloy, and they are wonderful, loving, caring people. I don't think they should be denied something as wonderful as that.'

Stephen himself was revelling in domestic bliss. 'I would love to get married to Eloy, I can't think of anything that would make me happier,' he said. 'At the minute, I'm really waiting for him to pop the question. I think marriage is a great thing and, if two people are in love and intend to be responsible to their commitments, then why shouldn't they tie the knot?'

Sadly, Stephen and Eloy would not last the course, though, for more upheaval lay ahead.

CHAPTER EIGHT

A CHANGE OF PLAN

As 2000 drew on, Stephen was beginning to think seriously about future plans. His solo career wasn't going quite so well as he'd hoped – indeed, of all the boys, only Ronan would really make it as a singer out on his own – and Stephen was now starting to assess the opportunities in front of him.

'I always have three things I plan to do in a year and over the next year I wanted to be in a musical, be involved in TV and write a theme song for a film,' he told one interviewer. 'I went to see *Billy Elliot* on my own and sat in the theatre and wondered what a movie about ballet was going to be like.

'As I sat there and watched it, I realised I could relate to that character. Like Billy Elliot, I grew up in a poor background. It was a real struggle, so the film struck a chord with me. It's a film about believing in yourself, following your goals and achieving your dreams. We knew what it was like to struggle as a family and my parents wanted me to finish school then get a job. I was determined to be successful in the entertainment business, whether it was singing, dancing or acting.'

And, besides, Stephen had certainly made the right contacts. 'I know Andrew Lloyd Webber quite well,' he continued. 'He always sends me Christmas and birthday cards. They asked me to be involved in the musical *The Beautiful Game*, but there wasn't time; I was involved in my album at the time.

'We're in talks at the moment to do *Billy Liar*. This run is being shown on the West End and then Broadway. Imagine that, little me from Sheriff Street in Dublin on Broadway! I'd love to do it, I love musicals – I saw *Cats* when I was 13 because they happened to give out free tickets to kids in my area. No one was interested in musicals there, but as soon as I saw *Cats* I was hooked. In a way, I didn't want to grow up having to scrape by – I wanted to be comfortable. Where I came from was a rough area, lots of thefts and people on drugs, and I didn't want anything to do with it. I wanted to get out of there.'

He was by now spending most of his spare time with Eloy in Amsterdam, where civil partnerships were already legal. As such, observers were beginning to wonder whether he and Eloy might be getting ready to tie the knot. 'That's another rumour,' said Stephen. 'I spend a lot of time there because Eloy's family are from there, but my family is in Ireland: I'm close to my family, especially my sister, and I couldn't not see her.

'We've sold the house and we are just waiting for a nice apartment to come up in Dublin. I love it there. I haven't been asked by Eloy but we have talked about marriage. I'm not in any rush and neither is he. If it happens, it happens. When it all does, everybody will know, but I have no wedding ring on my finger. It might be three years down the line or sooner, if we get a kid.'

Indeed, Stephen could not stop talking about his desire to have a child of his own. 'I'd love a kid,' he declared. 'The way I look at it, I've been given a fantastic opportunity. I've been to more countries in the last couple of years than most people get to see in a whole lifetime; I've experienced so many things and so many different cultures. I've made money. I'm very content and very happy.

'I'd like to adopt a kid rather than have my own kid. It doesn't matter what race, just to give the kid a chance, put the kid through college and give a lot of love – we have a lot of love to give. I feel I really would know how to bring up a kid and I would love to.'

As for people who objected on the grounds that he was gay, Stephen had this to say: 'That's ignorance. You see so many stories of kids who are in horrible situations and yet they make it so hard to adopt. Some kids have no parents and live in orphanages. I wouldn't like a child through a surrogate mum – I would just like to adopt the baby. But at the moment we have two dogs and we can hardly take care of them because there is so much travelling. We'd have to be dedicated to the child and give the child a lot of time.'

But there was another reason why some people objected – the strange notion that being gay might somehow turn others the same way. 'It's rubbish to think that Eloy and I will turn the kid gay!' said Stephen. 'That's something you either are or you aren't, and you would know that from a certain age. We would never try to influence the child. We would be very open about the situation and explain things.

'Children don't have things explained enough, which is wrong. I believe parents should be open to children – at a certain age, of course. You have to let children make up their own minds about their sexuality. I knew from the age of 14, but I think I was born gay.'

And he was certain at that point that Eloy was his life partner. 'Eloy is incredible-looking,' he said. 'The first thing that attracted me to him was his looks. I was like, Wow! I thought he was a cool guy, really tall and a good-looking geezer. It was just his way. We clicked and found out that we had so much in common; we learned from each other.

'We're very happy and just want to be seen as a normal couple. Some couples last a year or six months and then split, we want to be together forever.'

Alas – it was not to be.

Nor was his solo career. Stephen's first single got to No. 3 and the accompanying album (both titled *New Beginning*) reached No. 4, both respectable figures, but nowhere near what he had achieved with Boyzone. His second single only made No. 11, despite being in the *Billy Elliot* film.

'Stephen hasn't lived up to expectations,' remarked an industry insider. 'He's a lovely guy and a hard worker, but people haven't liked his music and he hasn't sold enough singles. Nobody likes to be ruthless, but artists have got to sell.'

Indeed, stories began to circulate that his record company was thinking of dropping him.

Nor were matters on track in other ways. Stephen had not managed to land a part in the most recent *Harry Potter* movie, although he seemed to take this in good humour. 'They have not given me a part, so I'm saying to everybody, "Don't go to see the movie because it's going to be terrible,"' he said.

To make matters worse, there were rumours that Ronan was up for the lead in the stage version of *Billy Liar*, too.

In all, life was not exactly going according to plan. The other ex-Boyzone members were also finding it tough. 'I'm not a good singer,' said Keith, who had just had a less-than-successful stint as a television presenter. 'I'd be the first to tell you that. I'm a good entertainer. I was pants! [at interviewing] Other bands looked down their noses at me because I was the interviewer.'

And then it really came out: 'I miss the lads more and more, to be honest,' he admitted. 'When you started to get a little bit lonely, you were never on your own – you always had someone with you. When I saw Ronan walking on stage at the MTV Awards, I was in bed in London, feeling lonely. It's hard that way. There's been a lot of stuff about me and Ronan and other fellas in the band; all I can say is that we are as close as brothers. We've been together for seven years.'

But they weren't together now. However, Keith and Shane were able to poke fun at themselves: they had teamed up to do the Milli Vanilli number 'Girl You

Know It's True', at least partly because Milli Vanilli were notorious for not singing their own songs.

'I remember a Cockney lad rang up a radio show and said, "Respect to the two big lads at the back who never sang a note and just took the money,"' Shane recalled. 'I thought that was funny, even though we did sing. We're releasing the Milli Vanilli song because people think we didn't sing. It's about mickey-taking, it's just a buzz. We're taking the mick out of ourselves and other people.

'I'm not very passionate at all when it comes to music. What I do is a job: I'm in a boy band, but I'm into hip hop. I wouldn't buy a Boyzone record, but I love being an entertainer. But me and Keith will never, ever, do a ballad.'

In the event, the single flopped – not least because it wasn't considered good enough to get national airplay on the radio. And Ronan continued to be the only one to be making his way.

Not that some of his band mates were helping themselves. All of Boyzone had been praised for their support for Stephen when he came out, but Shane rather put his foot in it when he commented, 'I've got no problem with gay people, but I'd rather be shot in the head than have sex with another man!' Tactful it wasn't, although, in fairness, Shane (who had by now separated from Easther) also said in another interview, 'One of my best mates in the world is gay and that's Stephen Gately. I'd never let anyone have a pop at him, I'd be there to stop it.'

Given all the unhappiness at being on their own, it was no surprise that, at the end of 2000, Keith announced the band was beginning to talk about doing another tour. Indeed, it appeared everything was pretty much settled. 'We have not split up and these live concerts are going to prove it to the fans once and for all,' he declared. 'I spoke to Ronan Keating about it last night. He is enthusiastic and so is everyone else. There's been a lot of rubbish about us breaking up recently, but we're still together.

'We will be playing in big arenas, including the Point in Dublin and the Odyssey in Belfast. We think there will be around ten concerts, hopefully more. We will probably announce the tour officially on a special occasion like St Pat's or Valentine's Day. But it will be a big day for us – the day when we tell the world that we are still together.'

Then there was the rub – this wasn't an official announcement. The boys had been talking about it and everyone, most crucially Ronan, was feeling enthusiastic, but the deal was not done and dusted. It was just that everyone was finding it a little harder to be on the outside than they'd thought they would. Keith admitted as much.

'I've felt a bit sorry for myself since January to be honest, but I always pick myself up again,' he said. 'I made a mistake by taking the band for granted. As soon as we went our separate ways, I started to miss it. There have been very hard times for me, especially when I've seen Ronan performing at awards on his own, without the rest of us.

'It makes you miss the buzz of being right at the centre of the pop world. There is nothing that can replace the amazing feeling of being on stage with the band. I have missed it – much more than I ever thought I would.'

At this stage, however, everyone was still on good terms and a meeting was planned in a London hotel. It was perhaps a little unwise of Keith to talk about it all so much, but he was clearly just eager to get back together with his friends and couldn't contain himself.

'We were going to meet in Dublin, but we decided to change it to London just so we can have a little more privacy,' he continued. 'This is the first time we have all been in the same room since January, so we're aware that there could be a big media frenzy around it. We're just going to have a few drinks, something to eat and make some plans. Everyone wants to talk about the tour so we've set a date to get things organised by.'

But not everyone was convinced. Brian McFadden, lead singer with Westlife, had recently had a conversation with Ronan, and he rather doubted it would all be that simple.

'They're well gone – I can't see them getting back together,' he commented. 'I don't mean that in a bad way, I love Boyzone, but Ronan has reached a stage where he has to focus on his own future, and Ronan *was* Boyzone in my opinion.'

Indeed, Ronan himself had already stated publicly, 'I can't really see us touring. I have to concentrate on my solo career and I have America to think of too.'

Even Mikey was sounding a little unsure. 'It's been done already – you've had Take That, you've had Boyzone, you've had Westlife,' he said. 'I wouldn't be interested in trying to re-create that again. My solo career is more important to me now, even if it means I have to make do with just a few hundred fans. I don't care. I'm now getting to write my own songs and make the kind of music which I enjoy.'

Industry observers were also extremely dubious about the chances of a reunion.

'Ronan is possibly trying to appeal to an older market now,' said Ian McLeish of the website Worldpop. 'With Boyzone, he felt he was being made to sound too young. There was a feeling around the Boyzone camp that his image was getting too mature for a young audience. He is a very level-headed lad, who sounds ten years older than he is. The first solo single was funkier than Boyzone and now he has decided to have a bit of a laugh. He is enjoying shouting his mouth off, whereas, with Boyzone, everything was very controlled.

'He is now trying to appeal to people of his own age. A lot of people thought he was wise beyond his years in Boyzone, so it's unlikely he'll go back. He was in one of the biggest boy bands in the world and could have been living it up and partying, but was going to bed early to be responsible.'

By now, some real bitterness was beginning to emerge. Shane had started to indulge in some regular outbursts, upsetting people by swearing on television, criticising the Irish and, worst of all, having a pop at Ronan. 'Bloody Ronan threw me out of Boyzone because I wasn't gay enough – it's as simple as that,' he stated at one point, a bizarre claim that no one could understand. 'He was always a prat and I'm happy to tell you I haven't seen or spoken to him for weeks. Do you know what? I think maybe the next time I see that jumped-up prick I'll give him a damned good slapping!'

Clearly, disappointment, or something like it, was taking its toll.

While all this was going on, perhaps wisely

Stephen was keeping his head down. He wasn't finding the solo life all he'd expected, but to openly attack Ronan was not the way to get him on board for a tour. And so he contented himself with promoting his own record and confirmed what was not now happening, rather than what was. 'There were plans to do a film, but it doesn't look like it's going to happen now,' he said. 'When they eventually get round to making the film of my life, I'd like Tom Cruise or Brad Pitt to play me, but they'll probably get Mr Bean.'

Then came another blow – there had been hopes that he might play 'I Believe' at the Oscars ceremony. In the event, it was not even nominated for Best Song.

In March 2001, matters came to a head: Ronan refused to sign up for the tour. The other four had wanted to, but, without him, it was impossible. Bad tempers spilled out again. 'We had everything planned,' said a livid Mikey (who wasn't the only one to get angry). 'There was a lot of money on the table and we were all looking forward to it, but Ronan suddenly pulled out and we don't know why. Now none of us has any room in our diaries for at least two years, so the fans are in for a long wait.'

Keith attempted to be a little more diplomatic, but he was clearly livid, too. 'Four of us were very happy to do a tour in November this year,' he said in a radio interview with Dublin's 98FM. 'We promised the fans more concerts and it's what we all wanted to do. Ronan is the chief singer but he doesn't want to do the tour, so it won't happen. But I hope one day the tour will happen. And I hope Boyzone members will remember where they came from and decide it is the right thing to do. If a tour doesn't happen, I will probably have to go back to picking up golf balls or selling Christmas logs.'

Everyone, however, was fine with each other, he said, continuing, 'If any of the lads from Boyzone called me in the morning, looking for a favour, I would have no hesitation in trying my best to help them out. They are my dearest friends. All I can say is that there's a lot of successful members of Boyzone doing very well at the moment, but if any of them called me, I would be more than happy to do a favour for them.'

It was obvious, though, that he was very upset. 'The DJ Niall Boylan could see what was going on in the studio: Keith came across as being very complimentary and chummy towards Ronan,' an observer in the studio said. 'But what listeners didn't see are the gestures he was making with his hands while he praised him. While telling listeners what a gentleman Ronan was, he made hand gestures about him which were not very flattering, to say the least. That suggested to me that relationships between them are definitely strained.'

And Keith couldn't help himself when a caller claimed, 'I'm a good friend of Ronan.'

'Oh are you?' said Keith. 'I didn't know he had any good friends.'

Louis Walsh knew what he thought. 'Boyzone have passed their sell-by date and there is no going back,' he said. 'You have to let something like that go.'

Stephen, wisely, refused to be drawn. Instead, it was reported that he was helping Noel Sullivan, of the newly formed band Hear'Say, cope with the pressures of newfound fame.

'Everything has been getting on top of Noel since the band formed,' said a source from Polydor, the record label they both shared. Then, a few weeks ago, he met Stephen and the two of them got on like a house on fire. Noel has turned to Stephen because he's been through it all himself and he feels comfortable with him. Stephen has been in the public gaze since Boyzone were formed seven years ago and is well qualified to give Noel some really good advice.'

Stephen was preparing for a new record release – 'Stay', out in April 2001 – and made no bones about how keen he was to tour. 'I'd love to do a tour – I'd sign a contract tomorrow,' he admitted. 'And I still haven't heard that we've split up, so I imagine we're still together.' And his determination to do well was such that he turned down the chance to appear in *Billy Liar* in New York: he knew now that he had to stay in Britain to promote the song, because he was now seriously in need of a big hit.

He was also looking after his appearance. 'I've been on a diet and I've given up alcohol,' he said. 'I'm trying to look after myself. I used to drink a lot with the guys, but it's been nearly five months and I feel a lot better.'

Meanwhile, one person who most certainly was enjoying going it alone was Ronan. He had a new single out, 'Lovin' Each Day', but was sounding surprisingly conciliatory towards his erstwhile band mates, given some of the things they'd been saying about him.

'I'd love to do something with Boyzone again,' he protested. 'I don't want to call it a day with the group and I still have a great relationship with the lads. But, if some people want to close the book on Boyzone, there's not a lot I can do about that.

'I haven't turned my back on anybody. My phone is on for the guys to call me at any time, but they've got to understand that I'm up to my eyes in it at the moment. I'm out promoting my solo album and my wife has just had another child – they should know what it's like. To say I've turned my back on them is absolute crap! I'd love to front Boyzone again, just not right now.'

He was, in fact, going to do so – but not for another seven years.

Unlike the others, Ronan was relishing time on his own. 'It's nice to have the artistic freedom to do exactly what I want,' he admitted. 'My new single was written by Gregg Alexander of the New Radicals, who is the man of the moment right now. We have a wonderful relationship – a bit like Elton John and Bernie Taupin – and I'm very lucky to have him. As a solo artist, I had to get away from the whole teen-pop Boyzone thing. Now, I've been welcomed into circles I'd never have been invited to with Boyzone.'

And, although he missed his band mates, the experience was making him stronger, too. 'In the band, we were able to distribute the weight and the worry across five sets of shoulders,' he said. 'There have been many times in my solo career when I looked over my shoulder and the guys weren't there. But, as a person, I've become stronger. If something good happens now, it's because I've made it work.'

He sounded very different from his erstwhile band mates – but then, that was hardly surprising. Unlike them, he was doing extremely well.

At least Stephen was still happy with Eloy. 'We have a park just round the corner, where we walk the dogs and feed the swans, and that's breathtaking,' he told one interviewer. 'And our land is on water, anyway. We have a boat, so we go off down the canals with the dogs and a picnic on sunny days and read our books. I always have to have incense and sometimes I light 40 candles a night. We used to be addicted to Jo Malone. She does these scented candles, and the smell! The grapefruit one is to die for!'

As the relationship intensified, Stephen began to doubt he would ever return to Ireland – and he was right, although not in quite the way he imagined. 'I've really settled down in Amsterdam and I regard the place as my home,' he said. 'I'll never forget about Ireland and I'll always return to see my friends and family. But, after I came out and admitted that I was gay, I needed a new start. It's a different culture in Holland, but I feel really at one with the place.'

'Stay' got into the charts at No. 13, which to put it bluntly wasn't good enough. Shortly afterwards came the news that Stephen had known, deep down, was on its way: he was dropped by his record company, who at least did the deed when he was on holiday, so he wasn't forced to comment. 'Stephen is no longer with us,' said a spokesman for Polydor. 'We had a good relationship and wish him all the best with his future career plans.'

Everyone involved tried to put a brave face on it, but in truth this was a terrible blow. 'This is devastating for Stephen and he is gutted,' said a source. 'He wanted to prove that he could survive in the pop world without the rest of the Boyzone lads. He's very sad that it didn't work out, but he won't be giving up his dreams.'

Stephen now had to decide what to do next. One option was to stay in the music business, but play a role behind the scenes. After all, Ronan had done it, in bringing on Westlife.

'Stephen has been assessing all the different possibilities and he'll be taking time out at home in Amsterdam,' revealed a friend. 'But he is very interested in starting his own boy band similar to Boyzone. He has all the experience of being in a pop group for seven years and he knows how to play the game – there's even a possibility he will be in it himself. He knows it won't be easy to find the talent: there are also a lot of good boy bands already out there.'

It was easier said than done, but Stephen at least was maintaining his cool, something Shane was increasingly unable to do, coming out with yet another broadside against Ronan. 'I don't mind any man who wants to step out and do his own thing,' he declared. 'We all decided to take a year out. He said he was going to do a solo album, then come back to do our tour. If we had known he wasn't coming back, we could have got on with our lives. That's why I'm pissed off. He's still saying we could get back together and tour, but, as far as I'm concerned, it's not going to happen.

'We'd have made it in America. We're Paddies, man! Americans love Paddies! The big bucks were going to roll in, that was my next house in the Caribbean. I was looking to the future and it didn't happen. It's Ronan's fault, no one else's. We all wanted to do America so all four of us feel like this. I just hope I never run into him again – I will put him down so hard.'

Nor was Keith very happy. 'They treated me like a bloody nobody,' he said. 'Ronan wants the limelight to himself. I have had plenty of sleepless nights and tears because of him.

'The last time I spoke to him, I said, "Have a successful career, pal, and forget about me." Why would he call me? He's got his entourage and Ronan plays God. He doesn't need me with new friends like Elton John!'

And from Mikey: 'Ronan doesn't phone, he doesn't write and he doesn't call. It took five people to make Boyzone and five people to make Ronan Keating. I just don't know – people change.'

Ronan was singularly unmoved by it all, and, canny

player that he was, had an eye on the longer term. He might not have been planning to tour with Boyzone any time soon, but he would certainly not rule it out for the longer term.

'You know, I heard the other day what Shane said and I was pissing myself laughing,' he admitted. 'I don't know where the hell he gets that stuff from. Shane was never thrown out of any band – Boyzone never broke up and we never threw anyone out. Shane's got a bone of contention with me and he thought he'd pick on something.'

And so, the message was never say never and the more circumspect Ronan would one day indeed be proved right.

Meanwhile, Stephen still contemplated his immediate future. A couple of years previously, he had voiced the character of Blackavar in the television series *Watership Down*, and now there were discussions about him appearing on the BBC cult comedy *Absolutely Fabulous*, which was returning for a new series in 2001.

In the meantime, Ronan continued to tease, holding up the possibility of a reunion without ever committing to it. Given what his former friends had been saying about him, he also proved remarkably able to rise above it all, saying that they'd all met up and the situation was calming down.

'The past is the past,' he insisted. 'There were a few misunderstandings in the past, but that is now behind us. We all sat down and discussed the band and the future and realised just how big things were in the past. And we've all spoken about putting the band back together for a tour and there is a chance we will do that soon.'

Ultimately, Stephen was the only one who had managed to stay out of this war of words, but he'd suffered his own disappointments and his future was looking as insecure as that of his former band mates. He did have the option of acting, however, and this was an option that he was going to take, but the strain was taking its toll and he was about to plunge into a depression that would last for about two years. Nor was his relationship with Eloy as stable as he'd once thought it was.

Stephen's life was to be a rollercoaster for some time yet.

CHAPTER NINE

SEPARATE WAYS

It had not been a very good time for Stephen since Boyzone started to pursue their separate projects – as they all kept telling everyone, they had not actually split up. And matters rapidly got worse. The problems had been taking their toll on Stephen and now they were affecting his personal life, too: at the beginning of 2002, after nearly three years together, he and Eloy split up. After yet another blow, Stephen returned to Dublin to stay with Michelle for a while.

'Stephen is upset by what has happened, but things move on,' said a friend. 'They are still good friends, but have gone their separate ways now. Things had become strained between them and there was always a lot of pressure in their relationship because of the fame. They have had almost three happy years together but they have been in the public gaze all the time. They both come from the music business so they knew what to expect; they just need time to sort out their feelings now and get on with things.

'He is really just taking it day by day and returning to normality as much as possible. Stephen's looking at new properties and is considering a move back home. They had been living together for so long that it's going to be a big adjustment for both of them.'

It was indeed. Not only had he lost his stable home base, but Stephen also now had to juggle the commitments of work while finding out just what he wanted to do.

'Stephen is commuting to London each week, where he is working on new music projects,' revealed the friend. 'He just wants to get on with things now and focus on relaunching his career. All of 2001 was pretty much a nightmare year for Stephen and he is starting afresh now. Eloy has been there to support him after he was dropped by his record company; but they started drifting apart and that was really the final nail in the coffin. It all came to a head around Christmas and they decided to remain friends but call it a day. Everyone who knows them has been really shocked by this because they were such a close couple. They even talked openly of their dreams of adopting children together but everything changed so quickly.'

And, as if that were not enough, details of another

aspect of Stephen's life now came into the public domain: that he was not on speaking terms with his mother. However well intentioned her intervention might have been when Stephen came out, several years previously, he had taken it very much to heart and matters had still not calmed down between the two of them.

'Margaret is upset, but she knows Stephen will come around,' said a source. 'They are both very stubborn. He's her son and she's mad about him. Stephen is a very special and loving person too, but they can't seem to patch up their differences.'

At least he was back in Dublin for a time, but what happened all those years ago continued to rankle. 'Stephen was furious with his mam,' continued the source. 'He rang her the next day and told her she had no business talking to newspapers about him. He had admitted he was gay, but the things she said about how special he was to her were lovely. Unfortunately, Stephen didn't see it that way.

'She's lovely – only recently a fan arrived at the house and she invited him around for Sunday dinner. People are always calling in to her to ask her how he is. The rest of the family find it awkward that they are fighting – I just wish one of them would pick up the phone. Margaret is glad he's back in Dublin with his sister because it's a difficult time for him. We are hoping that the split from Eloy will make him think about things – life is too short. Margaret barely knows how he is after the break-up, but she just gets on with things. It doesn't mean she doesn't think about him every day.'

In fact, Stephen wasn't taking anything very well at all. The problems in his career, followed by ructions in his personal life, had taken their toll and he was suffering from a serious bout of depression.

'The split has hit Stephen bad,' said a friend of the family. 'They were in love and now that's all gone. He's always been a rock for the family and has so much drive and ambition, but I'm afraid he just won't respond to anything. He's locked himself away in his bedroom and won't take any calls. We're all there for him but he's just shut everyone out and we're really worried about him.

'It's not only his split from Eloy that has depressed him. He was dropped by his record label and Boyzone's break-up didn't help. Stephen had everything and now it seems he's lost it all. We're all keeping our fingers crossed for him. He's got to snap out of this and get back on his feet.'

Stephen was to do just that, but it was tough for a while. He admitted that he was hoping for a reunion. 'I have hopes it will sort itself out and we'll be together in the future – I like to think that, I have hope in my heart,' he said sadly. 'My heart is broken. It's a very tough subject to talk about.'

He was nothing, though, if not a fighter, and so he gave an interview, saying that he was looking forward to the future. After all, there was all to play for. 'I've been through a tough time lately and at one stage I thought the pain would never end,' he said. 'But I'm getting there and am involved in talks for performing in a musical in London's West End. I can't say which one just yet, but you'll be the first to know when I've signed!

'I really miss performing, which is one of the things that has got me through my dark days, but now I'm thinking positive and am ready to face the world again. I can't wait! Yes, I was bad. I think sometimes you go so low that the only way is up because there's only so much you can take. You've got to stay strong, otherwise you end up feeling sorry for yourself and that's no good to anyone.'

It was a wise attitude to take, and he soldiered on. But there was certainly no sign of peace breaking out between the erstwhile band members: there was still some bitterness there. Louis, no less, felt the need to stand up and defend Ronan.

'The press here [in Ireland] want to give Ronan a hard time,' he said. 'They do not want him to succeed; they think he's got too big for his boots. I can see where they get that idea. Sometimes he says the wrong things and is a bit too flash, but he's a good guy. It's early days, watch him – he'll surprise us all yet. There's no tragedy here.

'Ronan is very happy, very secure, but he's very ambitious and wants to be King of the Castle. He's 25, and he can be Cliff Richard, if he wants – but he doesn't want to be Cliff Richard. He wants to be a bit more edgy. I think he's great doing MOR ballads – I think that's what he's good at. Looking for respect for making pop music is silly; he should never have said that. All you should want to be is successful. Nobody is ever going to give Ronan respect here, nobody respects anybody here: nobody respects Enya or Clannad or Van, or even Bono here. They get it in America, and everywhere else, but not here. Get used to it!'

Nor was Ronan showing much desire to pour oil on troubled waters. He had been fairly diplomatic for some time, but was becoming less so, perhaps needled beyond endurance by Keith's constant jibes. 'I don't think we'll ever get together again,' he said. 'I don't know what any of them are doing. Sadly, we have grown apart and moved on. We don't speak to each other any more. We all made the same decision: I was the one who was successful. I'm not bitching, I hope they do well with their careers, or whatever.'

For someone who wasn't bitching, this sounded pretty close to the bone.

The rest of the boys continued to brood about what to do next. There was talk of a tour without Ronan, though, in truth, it could never have worked. Ronan himself, inexplicably, appeared to be trying to cultivate a wilder image, talking about how he'd trashed the odd hotel room and that life with Boyzone was like 'one long stag party' – rather at odds with what had gone before.

He might have been feeling a little sensitive about something else. The other four boys had made a television documentary about the end of Boyzone (by this stage, no one was expecting a reunion) and there was some considerable bitterness from them. Titled *Smash! The Story of Boyzone*, this was to be a no-holds barred analysis of what had gone on.

'We were finishing the European tour and Ronan came in and he said, "Listen, lads, I want to talk with you,"' Keith recalled. 'The hair stood up at the back of my neck and he said, "I wanna do my own stuff. I want to go into my own solo career just for about 12 months," he said. "Just take one year out." Myself and Shane were blue in the face going, "You're mad, let's ride it out for a couple of years and then you can do what you like!" The last night on stage, I kinda knew this is the last time that I'll perform with these boys. And right enough it was.'

And the real bone of contention continued to be the

tour that never was. 'Everybody was in agreement that we would come back one year later to probably put a new album out, a new single and go on tour again,' said Mikey.

Even Stephen, who had largely kept his own counsel so far, chipped in. 'I think Ronan just wanted to break into America and to be a really, really big star,' he said.

And then, according to Keith, there was the financial aspect of it all. 'Ronan loved to spend money and he spent a lot more than the rest of us, and in signing a solo deal he was going to get a fantastic advance,' he added.

As for Shane: 'I thought we were going to have a year out and come back and do one album and one tour, and continue on as Boyzone. Nobody has said anything to do with whether Boyzone has completely split up. Fans don't know, press don't know, nobody knows.'

Another issue, and one that clearly continued to rankle, was that television appearance on Gay Byrne's show all those years ago. The boys took the opportunity to say what they thought about that, too. 'I think Gay Byrne just done what the people expected him to do – which was to take the piss out of these six lads that looked like total gobshites, you know,' said Keith. 'He came out, and, from the word go, he was so condescending. We didn't even notice. For the first three years after that, I used to cringe every time I saw it, but now when I look at that I have a feeling of proudness because you kinda were that crap at one stage, and, with enough determination and hard work and luck, look at what you can achieve.'

It was certainly the best way to view it, though Shane was a little more abrupt: 'When we got to the studio, Gay Byrne... basically said we could not go on the TV show unless we were going to perform for him, so now it is in our hands to find something to do in an hour.'

So, just how did Ronan come to be the group leader? After all, he didn't start out that way. 'Myself and Stephen sang the first song, which kind of really launched us in Ireland as a band, and then after that I don't know how it happened at all, I really and truly don't,' revealed Mikey. 'But, for some reason, Ronan just started becoming the front person. Him and Louis got on well together and obviously Louis was the manager, and, the next thing you know, Ronan was singing everything. And it wasn't because nobody else could, but none of us really know the reason for that one. Maybe it's better left up to the imagination than anything, you know.'

Of course, Stephen's own preoccupation was that his secret would be found out. 'I was always doing press and waiting for that question, you know – "Are you gay?" – and I'd be there shitting it,' he admitted.

'And I'd be there, God, that bloke's gonna ask me or she's gonna ask me; I was really stressed out for a good time. I didn't want to mess up the career of a group just because of my sexuality. It sounds hilarious now, but at the time that's how I felt.'

But Ronan refused to take all this lying down and was quick to reply, and not particularly kindly: 'We had equal opportunities and for me it was a case of grabbing everything that was going. When Boyzone took a year off, we all went off to do our separate things. Myself, Stephen and Mikey all had records out. But the difference was mine took off and theirs didn't. So, a year later I was still busy promoting my record while they were left with nothing to do. I was never the biggest spender in Boyzone. Sure, I made more money and spent it too, but that's because I wrote some of Boyzone's hits like "Picture of You".'

Louis Walsh, who had not taken part in the programme, was also getting rather fed up. 'I just wish Stephen, Mikey, Shane and Keith would get on with their lives,' he said. 'Ronan Keating carried Boyzone – he was the only person to be always in the studio while we were recording. For me, Ronan was like Roy Keane and David Beckham. I pushed him because he was the best and I only want to work with the best. Do these people not understand Boyzone is over? Like the Bay City Rollers, it's never going to happen again, the moment is gone.'

That, it turned out, was not quite the whole story, though.

At this point, quite unexpectedly, Keith attempted to try to calm everyone down. In the past, he had been extremely vocal in his feelings towards Ronan, but now, perhaps because his own future suddenly looked a lot brighter, he was prepared to let matters lie. In fact, he went on to have quite a successful career as an actor, and it was about to start with a stint in ITV's much-loved soap *Coronation Street*, playing barman Ciaran McCarthy, and this might have been making him feel a little more magnanimous.

'At this stage, it's become a tired old line to slag off Ronan and I'm blue in the face talking about it,' he stated. 'The way I look at it is that I'm nearly 28 years old and I don't want to go through my life being bitter. I dealt with his leaving Boyzone at the time it happened and from the bottom of my heart I really do wish Ronan every success in the world.

'I do not want – and I do not need – any conflict. My career is really taking shape in the way I want it to and I do not wish anybody else any harm. Life's too short, you know. At the end of the day, I'm very happy and secure in my own career and the last thing I want to be doing is slagging anybody off.'

He was not, however, quite as forgiving towards Louis, saying that the former manager's constant put-downs had taken their toll on his confidence. 'It took me a long time to have any respect for myself in terms of talent,' he revealed. 'For so many years, Louis put me down. Louis was always putting us down in front of other people – he'd hate to think you were getting a big head. He thought he was doing the right thing; he thought we were cocky, confident young men. He didn't realise we were insecure young fellas and that we looked up to him as the big boss.

'We were a very successful group and I deserved credit for part of that success. Not getting it helped kill my confidence. It wasn't solely Louis's fault: I needed to find confidence from somewhere. It's very difficult when you're standing on a pedestal all the time, but other people were giving me an awful lot more credit than I ever gave myself; they obviously saw something there that I wasn't allowed to. People told me I'd be great on TV, but Louis kept telling me I was crap at everything. We were great friends then and I said it to him, one friend to another. I asked him to give me a break because it was dwelling on me. To be fair to him, he did.'

But then came a return to the sniping. 'There's no bad relations between me and Ronan because there's no relations,' Keith went on. 'I'm lucky enough to have a fantastic friend in Stephen, an absolute gent. I can't travel to London without seeing Shane or he'd go mad; he's another great friend on a different level. Mikey only lives ten minutes down the road; we've all got a very amicable relationship. When anybody's in need, there's no problem. A phone call, and we're all there. It's just unfortunate he's not part of that.'

Stephen, meanwhile, visited Amsterdam and was hopeful of reconciliation with Eloy. But it was not to be. He was, however, exceedingly open. 'I'm still very much in love with him and we have talked a couple of times since splitting up,' he told one interviewer. 'I don't really like to talk about this but I can't deny he is a very special person. I won't be truly happy until we are back together – I would hate to think we can't sort the problems out. We are well suited and I have been lost without him. I miss him and hope we can meet up again soon. Things just went wrong between us, and I think we lost control a bit and forgot what it was all about.'

Part of the problem, of course, was that he'd had such a bad year. 'Basically, the record company decided to let me go and there was nothing really I could do about it,' he went on. 'Obviously, I was upset about the whole thing because the three singles did pretty well in the charts – none of them were failures. I tried not to let it get me down, but the truth is, it hurt a lot at the time. I went back to Amsterdam with Eloy and tried to have a bit of time and space. I wasn't the happiest person in the world. But all things happen for a reason and I guess this is just my way of dealing with it.'

He was adamant, though, that Ronan's success wasn't upsetting him. 'It didn't hurt me to see Ronan doing well because I want him to have all the success in the world,' he stated simply. 'The hardest thing to deal with is not being able to get enough people to listen to your songs – that hurts the most. I worked really hard on the solo album and, in the end, it didn't work out the way I wanted it to.'

By this time, Stephen had sold his Irish home and was living in London, which is where he would be based for the rest of his life. 'The place was too big for just me – it was a luxury that I could do without,' he admitted. 'I have an apartment in London that suits me just fine and I can get on with my work over there. I came back to recuperate in Ireland for a few months, but I need to be in London most of the time now.'

Indeed, his career would soon be heading in a very different direction. Like Keith, Stephen was to discover a new career in acting and, in the autumn of 2002, he began to explore a few options; it would not be long before he was ready to go public about it all.

'I can't say exactly what the show is, but I am very excited that I've been given a couple of offers,' he told one interviewer. 'I would only do the lead role but, thankfully, that's what the directors have in mind for me. The bottom line is I want to be on the stage and singing – that is what my whole life is about. All these stories in the press that I have turned my back on the industry are a load of rubbish – it is in my blood, I could never give it up.'

And he was taking comfort in something else, too. The fact that he was now openly gay had been of help to other young homosexuals, who saw him as a role model. 'I dealt with it,' he admitted. 'There were plenty of other 23-year-olds with a lot bigger problems in their lives than that; there is always someone worse off than you. It was the best thing I could have done, it was a brave thing for me.

'I get mail from gay men who have gone through that. If my coming out helped stop someone committing suicide, then it was worthwhile. I got a lot of letters from all walks of life. I tended not to mention it [in the early days in Boyzone]. I was a very young guy and there was nobody I could talk to. Of the people that surrounded me, there weren't many gay people at all.'

Louis admitted: 'We used to put him with girls, any girls in pictures. I'd put him on Ruby Wax's lap and there was a story about him going out with Ruby Wax. We did him with Mandy Smith, too.'

And did he feel bad about it? 'Not really, it got him some borrowed time.'

Stephen was also getting on with Louis again. 'He gave me an opportunity to change my life around,' he said. 'I'll always be thankful to Louis for that. I went out with Louis last week and we sat down and had a coffee – it was good to see him.'

And his new project had now been revealed to the world: in 2002, he was to take the lead in *Joseph And The Amazing Technicolor Dreamcoat*, with an initial run in Liverpool before the production moved to London. His life was also about to change because he'd made a new friend: Elton John. He returned home to hear a message on his answerphone that was to alter his life: 'Listen, Stephen, we feel that you're down,' the voice said. 'We're at our home in Nice – we want you to come down. Come and stay, if you want to.'

'It was great to hear that,' admitted Stephen some months later. 'I caught a flight two days later and went to stay with Elton and David. And the rest is just history. Elton and David have been a godsend to me – they've introduced me to their friends and they consider me to be a friend.

'It was all very intimidating at first, but I thought, What have I got to lose? They've been really supportive of me and they always phone up to see if

I'm OK. Elton has a sixth sense if there's something not right with someone and if they have problems – he's really in tune like that. He and David are two of the most generous people I've ever met; they always give a lot of time to everyone they are close to. That's what makes them special – they care about people.'

At the time, the friendship hadn't become public, but a sign that Stephen might be mixing in illustrious circles came when it emerged that he was one of the guests at celebrations for David Furnish's 40th birthday, held in Venice that October. Life really was beginning to look up.

He was also starting to accept that his relationship with Eloy was finally over. Though painful, at least it meant that he would start to be able to move on. 'Steve's beginning to realise that maybe they'll never get back together. He knows he's got to try and get on with life, but obviously still holds out hope for a reconciliation,' revealed a friend. 'One of the hardest things he's done in his life is to come out and, when he told the world he was gay, he felt such a relief. And in Eloy he really thought he'd found his Mr Right – he'd even spoken about how much he loved children and what great parents they would make. He's desperate to have him back in his life but in the meantime his work has become his life and he really wants to make it as an actor.'

Indeed, acting was becoming an increasingly positive side to his life. Rehearsals for *Joseph* were gathering pace and, at last, it looked as if Stephen's career was beginning to take shape again. 'Steve is excited about it, but nervous at the same time,' said a friend. 'Acting is quite a bit different from singing on stage with your mates.'

Perhaps so – but it was a challenge, and that was maybe what he really needed then.

The only fly in the ointment was the relationship with Ronan. Stephen had been more circumspect than his former band mates, but it was obvious that he had been hurt. 'I haven't seen Ronan for about two years, since the band did the last gig,' he revealed in early 2003. 'None of us have seen Ronan. He went off – that was in 2000. I saw him once shortly after that. We were really close.

'As for Boyzone, we never officially split and still haven't. I don't know what happened. Ronan was supposed to come back. He said, "Let's have a year and a bit to do our own thing." He was doing an album and I was doing mine. We said we'd get back together and do a new tour, a new album and a new single. We were all waiting for that to happen, but it never has. Socially, we've felt abandoned, too. There was a time when I was doing *The Pepsi Chart Show* and he didn't come over to see me when he could have. At the time we were all hurt, but I've got over it now. He's moved on – Boyzone was a stepping-stone for him. As it was for all of us, but more so for him.'

In many ways, Stephen sounded just as hurt about Ronan as he had been about Eloy – the mention that they had once been close signalled the distance between them was hitting him hard.

Meanwhile, *Joseph* opened at the Empire Theatre in Liverpool to excellent reviews. 'I'm quite nervous,' Stephen admitted. 'Of course I've done big shows. With Boyzone, I played in front of audiences of more than 60,000. But it's worse in front of a smaller audience. When it's more intimate, they can see every detail – that can be more scary.'

He had certainly been nervous, but his debut had gone well. 'It was very warming to see so many of them – it was a huge boost,' he said. 'Keith and Shane came to the show and said, "We didn't know you could sing like that." Physically, it's less demanding than Boyzone, but vocally it's tougher. I was so nervous on the first night that I drank a whole bottle of Bach's Rescue Remedy to calm me down. Unlike Boyzone, I am holding the whole show. I don't like getting things wrong. When I perform "Close Every Door", you can hear a pin drop in the house. It's so different to having thousands of girls screaming when you sing.'

It was also perhaps a relief to show people that he was still around. Stephen had gone through a fairly reclusive period, but he was back in front of the public, doing what he loved best. The transfer to the West End now assured, he loved every minute of his new life.

'I think people started to wonder where I had gone,' he conceded. 'The truth is, I was just taking things slowly after years on the road. I felt exhausted by the time Boyzone had finished and I didn't know where my life was going. But it's an amazing feeling to be back on stage again and get that feedback from the crowd. There were times when I wondered if I would ever want to get back on the stage again but I am loving every minute of it.

'I would like to keep a high profile in the music industry, in one way or another. I don't think I will ever be in a pop band again, but I wouldn't mind managing one and guiding them to the top. I have a lot of ambition still, so you're going to be seeing me around for a long time to come.'

CHAPTER TEN

TAKING STOCK

Starring in *Joseph* gave Stephen a tremendous boost. For all that he put a brave face on it, the break-up (or whatever it was) of Boyzone and his subsequent failure to carve out a solo career had been a tremendous blow but now he was clearly beginning to feel considerably better. Nor had his parting from Eloy helped. But time had passed and he was becoming happier again and able to reflect on his solo attempt.

'I wasn't surprised or hurt [about being dropped by the record label],' he admitted. 'I didn't push myself forward, but I don't regret it. I'm very proud of the album and the work, but it became a wrench to be away from home. There were many times when I'd get a flight from London to Amsterdam at 7pm, see Eloy and have to be up at the crack of dawn to get back to London. It was like that for a year. I also had to have a kidney stone removed. I wasn't looking after myself because I was too busy.'

Indeed, that was why he needed to have a period calming down. 'I had to stop and take care of myself,' he continued. 'My heart wasn't in the promotion, so I didn't give my record a chance. The record company wanted me to do so much work and I wasn't up for doing it. And what I did wasn't good quality. You have to be happy, and doing all the promoting wasn't making me happy. Having No. 1 hits is not everything. I'm just glad I came out as I am much happier now. It was such a relief and I suddenly had this great sense of freedom.'

He had also spent some time in Dublin, first with Michelle and then in a new flat. And he was pleased about that, too. 'I'd had six hard years or more on the road with Boyzone, so I needed to let my brain think and not just run with it,' he said. 'After joining the band at 17, I had to grow up very quickly. I needed the time for me – to do simple things. I had a lot of time off. People kept saying, "Aren't you bored?" But I wasn't. And I know I'll do it again after being in *Joseph* – but not for as long this time.'

He had found fulfilment in working on his new flat, too. 'It was good for me to do up the flat because it took my mind off things,' he admitted. 'I got quite down, but there was lots happening. It's good that you have emotions and let them out – it would have been weird, if I hadn't. I needed to go through a period of introspection, do nothing and be supported by my friends and family.

'Keith kept saying, "Come and see me and the kids." Shane and Mikey kept in touch – even Ronan rang me after the split with Eloy. I've got nothing but admiration for these friends because they helped me through, and I made some new ones – including Lulu, Sting's daughter and the Pet Shop Boys.'

Indeed, he was only too thrilled about that last one. 'Elton and David are a real laugh,' he said. 'Elton rang me up and asked me to perform in his charity show at London's Old Vic, with Kevin Spacey, Sting and Lulu. It was a great opportunity – so many things have come out of that first phone call.'

And, as far as Louis was concerned, Stephen remained as grateful as he always had been. 'I haven't spoken to him an awful lot, but we have bumped into each other,' he said. 'I will always be thankful to Louis because I wouldn't be here today without him. I don't feel that he dumped me or Boyzone – I could call him up tomorrow, if I needed to. He's getting people to come along to *Joseph*.'

However, although Stephen was so much happier

now that he was out of the closet, he was resisting suggestions that he was an icon of some sort. The singer Will Young had also recently announced that he was gay, something that was almost certainly easier after Stephen's experience, but he didn't want to take it any further than that.

'I just happen to be a gay person,' he said. 'I am not a role model, I am just me: I live my life how I live my life. If people want to say I have helped them in some way, fair enough. I got a lot of letters saying, "You've given me the courage to come out to my family." It is not an easy thing to do, it is very difficult – people shouldn't be pressured, they should do it in their own time and be supported.'

When *Joseph* opened in the West End, it again received glowing reviews. 'In this latest revival, it still seems fresh as paint,' wrote Charles Spencer in the *Daily Telegraph*. 'Rice and Lloyd Webber may have gone on to bigger things, but I don't think either of them have ever done anything better than this. Every song is instantly, infuriatingly memorable. The tone is light, indeed at times downright infantile (it was, after all, originally written for kids), and the whole improbable enterprise of a pop musical based on the Bible is blessed with the exuberance of youth.'

'I was thrilled to see former Boyzone star Stephen Gately take the lead in Tim Rice and Andrew Lloyd

Webber's timeless classic,' said Kevin Sullivan in the *Mirror*. 'Bill Kenwright's masterful production of this wonderful 35-year-old musical allows Gately full range to showcase his talents. The whole splendid exercise was great fun.'

'Presumably, Kenwright chose him because Gately, being smallish and very winning, could embody a conception of Joseph as the appealing runt of the litter who thereby won his father's heart and his brothers' jealous hostility,' observed Paul Taylor in the *Independent*. 'But the performer brings another dimension. He sings so well and is so amused and mischievously at ease with his persona – a kind of sexy Boy (next door) George whom you could introduce to your mother – that he makes all of the audience, of whatever persuasion, fall for him. And the gay overtones give scenes like the late reunion with the father a heart-wrenching *East of Eden* quality.'

It was very much Stephen's moment. One interviewer who met him commented on how very down-to-earth he was: 'I would never abuse what I have been given,' said Stephen. 'I came from nothing. Yeah, I went through bad times, but people do. People are out there dying of cancer, dying of AIDS. Kids are dying of leukaemia. I'm lucky. I'm healthy. I'm alive. I'm successful. I'm doing what I want to do.' And he knew exactly what he was talking about, having done some work with The Make A Wish Foundation. 'They [the children] may not be here next year. They may not be here next month.'

One thing was still not quite right, though: the separation from Eloy. It turned out that Stephen was not so over him after all – indeed, he was really pining for him. 'I would give anything – everything – to get him back,' he admitted. 'Eloy is a lovely guy, the love of my life. I'm still very much in love with him and I feel lost without him. Our split wasn't about him. It was about me doing promotions, me being away a lot and me not having enough time to be with him. I'd love to make amends and have him back.'

Alas – it was not to be.

His increased profile was, however, causing a few other problems – not least the fact that he had by now acquired a stalker. 'She ... sends me the most bizarre letters I've ever received in my life,' he revealed. Indeed, he was so concerned about it that he had arranged for increased security at all times. 'She posts me pictures, she sends me big locks of her hair, she says that I'm her Pinocchio. This woman posts me pictures of herself holding pictures of me and she's crying. And she's scribbled on the back of them: "Look, I'm crying for you, my Pinocchio." I've never met her and I don't want to. I'm scared – it's freaked me out.'

It was certainly an unpleasant situation, but his fellow cast members couldn't help teasing him on his 27th birthday. 'The cast got me this cake and they got her picture printed on it,' said Stephen. 'I couldn't believe it. Then somebody else decided to dress up as The Black Cat Zone and appear in front of me – it was all very freaky. It's a question of respect. As a fan you can enjoy being around a person, but you can't do that 24 hours a day because everyone needs time to themselves.

'If a fan stalked me they wouldn't respect my privacy and I wouldn't respect them. Yes, I have had to take one person aside and tell them they were going way too far.'

And, although friends were teasing him, in reality, this was no laughing matter. 'He hasn't been himself lately and he is watching his back all the time,' said a source close to Stephen. 'Stephen is a pretty laidback guy about meeting fans but now he is being very careful. Anyone who meets him has to be given approval beforehand. They don't want this lady just turning up out of the blue.

'There's a very small chance this woman would hurt Stephen, but you can never be too careful. It's hard to say whether she is in London or Israel. Nobody knows, so we have to be prepared. Since then he has been mobbed by fans wherever he travels and rarely ventures outside his home without a minder. The level of fame he has enjoyed over the past seven years is huge, but the downside of that is millions of people know who you are and there's always the chance that the odd fan could take it a bit too far. He is very anxious and is hoping that the letters stop, but there's no sign of it easing up yet. Until then, he's just going to have to keep alert and he's taken advice about extra security measures.'

In the meantime, other plans were afoot. For the first time, Stephen started looking for a home in London, the city in which he would end up living for the rest of his life. And the remaining members of Boyzone continued to discuss a reunion without Ronan, while matters remained bitter as ever there.

And then, in the summer of 2003, things really did begin to look up. Elton John and David Furnish had introduced Stephen to a friend of theirs, a computer-company mogul called Andrew Cowles. It wasn't long before the two were seen out and about together, not least at Elton's annual White Tie & Tiara Ball.

'It's early days, to be honest,' a bashful Stephen told one interviewer. 'We get on like a house on fire and spend most of our time at my flat in central London. Andy and I do all the normal things like eating out

Stephen Gately and
Andrew Cowles celebrate
their civil partnership
ceremony at the Goring
Hotel, London on
19 March 2006.

Above: Stephen waves goodbye after a secret Boyzone meeting at Universal Records HQ. The meeting in early February 2007 sparked rumours of a reunion for the first time since 2000.

Below: By November of the same year, Boyzone confirmed they were returning to the music scene while appearing on *The Late Late Show* in Dublin.

Above left: Stephen joined the cast of the second series of *Dancing on Ice*.

Above right: Wowing the crowd with his ice-skating partner Kristina Lenko.

Below: Other celebrities on the ice that season included Duncan James, Ulrika Jonsson and eventual winner Kyran Bracken.

Above: Boyzone perform together at the Childline Charity concert in Dublin. They were joined by *X Factor* runners-up JLS, Enrique Iglesias and The Saturdays.

Below: Stephen Gately and Boyzone helped to raise over £400,000 for Childline during the concert.

Stephen in his element, performing with Boyzone at Wembley Arena on 29 May 2009.

Above: Ronan and Stephen are all smiles at the Pride of Britain Awards on 5 October, 2009, Stephen's last public appearance before he flew to Majorca.

Below: Stephen taking a moment for himself during the final dress rehearsal for The Better Tour.

Above: Keith Duffy, Mikey Graham and Ronan Keating arrive at Palma de Mallorca airport after learning of Stephen's death.

Below: View of Stephen's apartment in Majorca, where he passed away.

R.I.P. Stephen Gately,
17 March, 1976 –
10 October, 2009.

and going for drinks, but we like nothing better than to stay in and chill.

'Since I've been doing *Joseph*, all I want to do is try to find time out to relax. We do two shows on Saturdays, which can be tiring but I love it. It's like being in Boyzone again, but not on tour every day. But when we do go out, we go to town and suffer from hangovers. We just clicked [when we met] and have been laughing ever since. I split from Eloy last year and had been just working flat out and not thinking about relationships. So when I met Andy it was like, Wow, I'm feeling something here and the feeling was mutual.'

It certainly was. Stephen made no secret of his desire to settle down and in August 2003, he and Andrew took part in a commitment ceremony in Las Vegas. But they hadn't told anyone in advance. 'Stephen and Andy went to Las Vegas on holiday and decided to attend a commitment ceremony,' his agent Grant Logan confirmed. 'They went to a chapel and the ceremony was carried out by a minister, although no rings were exchanged. Stephen and Andy have been together for a while now and they decided they were ready for more commitment. I don't think they told anyone else about it; they just wanted an intimate ceremony with the two of them. I have spoken to Stephen today and he says he is very happy.'

Sadly, at that point, however, Stephen was still not on speaking terms with his parents and they only found out about the ceremony from reading the papers.

Perhaps it was this newfound domestic happiness that was causing a distinct softening in his tone: Stephen was even willing to make up with Ronan. 'I haven't seen Ronan in a while, but I would like to meet up,' he said. 'It was true we weren't speaking. I speak to the rest of the guys except for Ronan and I look forward to receiving a call from him after the show.'

Unfortunately, shortly after this, Stephen and Andrew became involved in a physical brawl, although it appears to have been a one-off. The pair had been dining at The Ivy, London's favourite celebrity haunt, when they had a massive argument – it seemed that Andrew had been talking to another man. The row started in the restaurant and, after they were asked to leave, turned into a nasty incident on the street outside.

'The three of them came out of the restaurant and the bloke that was with Andrew shot off down one street,' said photographer Greg Brennan, who witnessed the whole scene. 'Stephen and Andrew were screaming at each other and Stephen was yelling something about him being out of order for being with this other guy. Andrew then cracked him and was really giving him a pounding; he was punching and kicking him. I had to do something – he was kicking him in the head, for God's sake. I managed to drag Andrew off and Stephen ran off back to the restaurant to clean himself up. There was some blood and he was crying his eyes out.'

Stephen was totally mortified, not least because it appeared he'd hooked up with the wrong man. He desperately tried to downplay it all, only too aware of the damage that pictures of the bust-up which appeared in the papers could cause. 'You know what it's like, boys will be boys,' he assured everyone. 'It only lasted a few minutes. We don't really know what happened. It was over something really stupid, but I just can't remember much of it.

'We were very tipsy and tired. We had just got back from Dublin after a long delay and we went home to change and then rushed out to dinner. We were with two friends. It's not fair as I whacked him first and he's getting the blame for whacking me. I started it. Let's just say we'll never do that again. We have laughed about it since but we both feel very silly. We're so embarrassed, but thankfully we're not banned from The Ivy.'

To take their minds off things, the pair hit the shops. 'We've had a lovely day together, shopping on Bond Street, and popped into Cartier to see if our wedding rings were ready to collect,' he continued. 'We are very happily married and have just bought a house in Highgate. We're moving in soon and are very serious about each other. Andrew isn't nasty, he's a sweet guy and we love each other so much.'

And certainly, the two were to stay together for the rest of Stephen's short life.

CHAPTER ELEVEN

MAKING AMENDS

By 2004, it was clear that Stephen was now settled in London for good. He sold his flat in Dublin and, with Andrew, settled happily into Highgate, a villagey area in North London, with plenty of green space and spectacular views out over the city. 'Things are great over there,' he told an Irish radio interviewer in Dublin. 'We go out together all the time. Anyway, because of work, we have far more friends living in London than Dublin these days.'

But the rumblings about a Boyzone reunion had never gone away and matters had by now calmed down so much that the other band mates were even on speaking terms with Ronan again. Indeed, given what they'd been through together in their formative years, it was a sadness that they had been at loggerheads for so long, but the past was well and truly in the past now, and they were all the best of friends.

'I'm not ruling out a Boyzone concert in the future because we are all talking again now,' said Ronan. 'It's great to be chatting and hanging out with all the lads again. We were like brothers. Like all families, you have feuds and fights and arguments, but ultimately you come back together and will always love each other. Who knows what the future holds, but I can definitely see us getting up there on stage together again.'

Funnily enough, it was Keith, who had been so keen for the reunion initially, who was sounding a cautious note. He had established a career for himself as an actor and was clearly concerned about being a member of a boy band once more. 'I've tried to shake off my Boyzone past and become a credible actor,' he said, after the boys had been spotted together for the second time in a week, this time at Palmerstown Stud Golf Course. 'I don't want to jeopardise my future. If my wife says a Boyzone reunion is a bad idea, it won't happen. My four old pals have just turned up to give me moral support. We have no plans at this moment in time to get back together; we just don't know yet. We're going to meet again next week. We'll sit down and see if it will work. We're all very open-minded about it.'

Whether or not they got back together, Stephen's new career was going well. He was delighted when he was cast against type as the Child Catcher in a new production of *Chitty Chitty Bang Bang* – everyone was always saying that he was the nicest man in show business and now he wanted a meaty part.

'This role is so unusual for me because everyone is used to me playing the cutey,' he admitted. 'It's great to get my teeth into an evil role. Everyone is scared of the Child Catcher – people will be running away from me now instead of asking for my autograph. They put a lot of make-up on to make me look older. It takes about two hours in total. My hubby saw the pictures of me and was in shock. I don't think he realised just what I was going to look like!'

There was some bemusement in the summer of 2004 when Louis admitted how he first got the boys a hit: by buying up the record himself and ordering the boys' families to do likewise. 'We got the band's families to buy some records and we got them all around the country,' he confessed. 'But it's the only record of any artist that I've bought, I want to tell you that. That's the absolute truth. It was their very, very first single. I wanted a No. 1 record.

'Riverdance was number one for like eight months. Wet Wet Wet had "Love Is All Around" out, so we had a lot of competition. We only bought a few hundred copies. We did buy them to try and get Riverdance and Wet Wet Wet out of the charts, but we couldn't – they were there forever.'

Indeed, the boys' first single only got to No. 3.

Stephen might not have wanted to be a gay icon, but he certainly got a mention in dispatches every time a new person came out. Already he had been cited as a person who made it easier for Will Young and now it was the turn of Mark Feehily from Westlife, another of Louis's bands, to admit that he too was gay.

'Well done, Mark,' said Stephen. 'What he's done will help thousands of other youngsters who fear the effect coming out will have on their families. I was in a similar position when I was in Boyzone, but coming out was the best thing I ever did. I got so much support from my friends, family and my fans. I was inundated with letters from people saying I had given them the courage to do the same. I remember one of the letters was from a young guy telling me he was suicidal until he read my interview and that had given him the courage to come out. I got flowers and letters of support from Sir Elton John, George Michael and The Spice Girls. Everyone was so supportive and I'm sure Mark will experience the same.'

As the Boyzone tour continued to be hinted at

(although it never quite materialised), Stephen continued to develop the other side of his career. He had found that he loved being on stage and enjoyed his stint as the Child Catcher just as much as he enjoyed playing Joseph: it seemed that this might be the future for him now. 'I am doing extensive acting classes at the Gate Theatre School,' he told one newspaper. 'I'd like to do straight acting, but I don't want to give up musicals as I enjoy singing far too much. My dream job would be a musical movie like *Moulin Rouge*! But I also fancy roles that people might not associate with me, such as an evil gangster.'

Now happy and settled, Stephen was doing his bit to give something back to the world that had given so much to him. He was already working with the Dream Come True foundation and now he became vice patron of the Missing Person's Helpline.

He was now also playing panto, having landed the role of Dandini at Bromley. 'I love the really horrible, nasty parts – they're much more fun,' he declared. 'The Child Catcher was great,' and then clearly jesting, said, 'Are you kidding me, getting paid to make children cry – it was fantastic!'

Speculation that Boyzone really were gearing up to that tour was ratched up another notch towards the end of 2005. Louis and Ronan also had a spectacular bust-up. 'Ronan betrayed me,' Louis raged. 'I gave everything for him and put him where he is now.' But now that a reunion was genuinely on the cards, he clearly decided he'd rather be friends. 'I'm ready to bury the hatchet. I'm ready to make up with Ronan, if he is – it's gone on too long now. I'll take his call if he rings me.

'I think the Boyzone tour would be a massive success and I would manage the lads again. It would be good for Ronan too. Take That have shown they can make a big comeback and it would be great to get Boyzone out there with them. Ronan and I have had our differences, but I don't see any reason why we can't work together and get Boyzone on stage again. You have to move on in life.'

Indeed, the success of the newly formed Take That was certainly a factor in what Boyzone would decide to do. When the four remaining Take Thatters, sans Robbie, decided to give it a go again, no one had any idea what the public's reaction might be. There were fears that no one would buy a ticket to the concert and that it would be an embarrassing flop. What happened, of course, was the comeback of the century: the band was, if anything, even more successful than they had been first time around. Now Boyzone were beginning to wonder if they could do the same.

Stephen was certainly all for it. 'There is talk of us getting back together and it's very exciting,' he said. 'All the lads are in favour of us doing something, even Ronan. He's still wavering a bit, but I think he will do it. We've come a long way.'

At the end of 2005, civil ceremonies for gay couples were introduced: Elton John and David Furnish were among the first to take advantage of the new law. Stephen took time out to attend the ceremony. 'We've given him a painting, but it's a very special kind of painting,' he teased. 'It's by a fantastic artist whose work is all, er, somewhat homo-erotic. It's funny, but a bit risqué. I don't want to go into too many details, if you know what I mean.'

But he was also looking to the future for it seemed as if the reunion tour was definitely going ahead, with Ronan now keen to take part, too. 'We had a long chat about re-forming and he is definitely in,' revealed Stephen. 'He said he can't wait to meet up with the rest of the lads again. We've also talked to Louis and he's keen. It's now just a case of agreeing a time when everyone is free. There's a lot of preparation to be done: I've started to hit the gym again to get a bit fitter for the dance moves. I've also started a diet to help me get in shape. As for the voice, there won't be a problem there as I'm classically trained. We can't wait to get out on stage again for the fans.'

Keith was also beginning to come round to the idea. 'Things with Ronan are never going to be the same as they were,' he admitted. 'We were all so close and spent so much time together, but the bubble burst when we split and you can't get that back. You shouldn't settle for second best either. We have moved on and all have different lives. But we didn't do too badly for five young guys from Dublin. I would never say never to getting back on stage with the lads but for me it would have to be with the six of us – the boys and Louis Walsh. It wouldn't be the same if one was missing, we were a team. But there could be one last farewell tour in us all right.'

In the meantime, Stephen and Andrew were also planning a civil ceremony, although Stephen did rather stun observers with the revelation that he'd had sex with women as well as men. 'I've bedded loads of girls,' he said. 'I've slept with girls, of course I have. When I was in Boyzone I slept with women, but, deep down, I knew I was always gay. There were always girls throwing themselves at us when we were in Boyzone. There was a lot of temptation there. They didn't just want your autograph, they wanted to sleep with you and marry you. I would never sleep with a woman again because I know who I am now and I'm completely happy with that.'

In March 2006, Stephen and Andrew became civil

partners. Of course, they had had a commitment ceremony is Las Vegas three years previously, but this time round, they wanted their relationship to be legally recognised and to have their friends there. The ceremony took place at the Goring Hotel, where the two exchanged diamond and platinum wedding bands, 'They wanted to get married to make everything official in the eyes of the law,' said a friend. 'The rules on gay weddings came in three months ago, but Andy and Stephen had already shown they were committed to each other by getting married in Las Vegas, but this ceremony means they are together legally as well as spiritually. And this time their family and friends were there to see them tie the knot too.'

Except, of course, that not all the members of the family were present: Stephen was still not getting on with his mum and dad.

The resultant publicity had one very unfortunate outcome, though. Stephen had been appearing as the Scarecrow in *The Wizard of Oz* at the Marlowe Theatre in Canterbury and had been thinking about buying a two-bedroom house in the town. However, he decided not to do so when he became the subject of a homophobic hate campaign. Indeed, thugs had been following him home from the theatre and he'd had to call the police.

'I've been abused by teenagers, and people have

been rude to me in shops,' said Stephen, who was taking it pretty calmly, all things considered. 'This is one of the reasons I got out of Dublin when I was younger and went to London.'

His immediate circle was disgusted. 'When Stephen first spoke about his sexuality, it took a lot of courage and I'll always love him for that,' said Ronan, who was now well and truly back in the fold. 'It's just sad that there are people in society who still hold these bigoted views. But I know Stephen will brush this aside, he's a very determined guy.'

Louis was equally appalled. 'I feel sorry for Stephen because, seven years on, he shouldn't have to put up with rubbish like this,' he said. 'The mindset is so outdated; these idiots really must have nothing better to do with their time.'

Although it had been very unpleasant for Stephen, he had at least one consolation: the public was firmly on his side. There might have been isolated incidents of homophobia, but the warmth with which he was usually treated and the outrage caused by these revelations showed that the world had well and truly moved on. Most people didn't turn a hair about the sexuality of a pop star – the numbers who were now coming out were testament to that.

And, by May 2006, it was very nearly official: a reunion was on the cards.

'It's the gig everyone wants to see,' remarked Louis. 'Boyzone was big and the fans are still out there. I believe they will tour again in 2007. Ronan is still a little reluctant, but I reckon he will be talked round. Ronan, Stephen and Shane met up for dinner on Thursday. The mood was good and I've no doubt a reunion was part of the conversation. I predict Boyzone will be back together and ready for an arena tour in 2007.'

Ronan was indeed on the verge of coming round, and it seems to have been a visit to a Take That concert that finally swung it. 'I saw Take That last Friday,' he said. 'They were completely brilliant. When the lads appeared, I hadn't heard a noise like it since Boyzone's last concert. I was feeling, This would definitely be nice again. I'm seeing the guys – we're probably going out for dinner on Thursday. We're hanging out and chatting, and that's all totally cool. So, never say never – but there's nothing planned.'

CHAPTER TWELVE

THE SHOW GOES ON

As the boys continued with behind-the-scenes negotiations about getting back on the road, it became clearer than ever that a re-formed Boyzone were set to be a huge success. They had, after all, scored six number ones and sold 10 million albums, while their tours had all been sell-outs. What was to stop them doing the same again? And some radical reassessments of the past were being made. Even now, over a decade on, Ronan was still plagued by the comments he had made about his virginity and appeared to want to set the record straight: that he'd been a bit of a bad boy, after all.

'I've tried it [dope],' he said. 'We went to Holland and, as everyone does, we tried it. I have to say it wasn't for me – I didn't enjoy it. But, on my mother's grave, I've never taken any hard drugs. I also made a massive mistake by saying I was a virgin at 16. It was true and I hope all kids are at that age, but when I went on the road there were lots of girls around and I lost my virginity early on.

'A lot of the time, there would be girls throwing themselves at me. I'd say, "No, no, no, I can't," because I was dating. Then I had a one-night stand for the first time and left my girlfriend the next day. I went through this brilliant stage of being with a different girl every other night. We weren't throwing TVs out of windows, but we'd be up until all hours drinking every night. There were parties after gigs, money thrown at us, all sorts.'

Stephen, meanwhile, was still involved with his solo work. He linked up with the operatic boy band G4 to record Boyzone's hit 'No Matter What'. 'Stephen is a big fan of G4 and hopes this will add to their album,' said a source.

He was also thrilled to be asked to play Tommy Tomorrow in a *Doctor Who* radio show on BBC7 titled *Doctor Who: Horror of Glam Rock*. 'When I was asked to do the show, I said yes immediately, because I was so excited,' he admitted. 'Plus, if I didn't do it, then my other half would kill me; he's a massive *Doctor Who* fan. And I'm really chuffed that I get to sing a song as well – that made it even better. It's a brilliant T-Rex-style glam-rock song that's really funky.'

'Stephen's got a really rare blend of charm and talent,' remarked the show's director, Barnaby Edwards. 'He produces an excellent performance and was a joy to have in the studio.'

Some other reassessments were going on, too. It had been seven years now since Stephen came out, and, other than the odd bit of nastiness such as the experiences encountered in Canterbury, the revelation hadn't had an adverse effect on his popularity at all. It was becoming apparent that his homosexuality had been something of an open secret, too. 'Everybody knew that Stephen was gay,' said Peter Loraine, former editor of *Top Of The Pops* magazine. 'One time in an interview, we asked them what they'd been doing at the weekend. They'd been car racing or at the pub getting hammered – but Stephen had been reading his horoscopes and getting into crystals.'

The circumstances in which Stephen came out were also now much more clear. Eloy had often been on the road with Boyzone, which is how one of the band's roadies found out what was going on and tried to sell the story to the *Sun*. 'They always had to be conscious, particularly on the road, of people seeing them,' said Caroline McAteer, who then handled publicity for the band. 'Eloy was obviously there, as other band members' wives and girlfriends were there; he was part of the tour party. But anyone outside of the band was going to start looking at it, thinking, Well, who's that guy?'

And it was she who advised Stephen on what to do when the revelations were put to her. 'You can't deny it because you'll be lying, so that's not even an option,' she told him. 'You either say, yes, I'm gay, or you say nothing at all. If you say nothing, they're just going to hound you. It's out there now – they'll follow you until they get that picture of you and Eloy, or until someone else sells them the story. It's only going to be a question of when. This is going to come out anyway. My advice is: you're better just saying it, and it coming from you. Otherwise it turns into some kind of sordid story.'

In the event, the press were far more sympathetic than they might have been just a few years earlier. Of course, Stephen had always got on well with many of them, which helped. 'We had so many young fans that the press had to deal with it in a sympathetic way,' he said. 'And partly because they knew that I'm sensitive. I was always friendly with everybody. I knew the press, I had done a lot of interviews – they knew me, and that I wouldn't hurt anybody.'

Indeed not. But, although Stephen was increasingly settled in his private life, he was beginning to accept that not all his dreams would automatically come true. 'I would love kids of my own, but you have to be realistic about these things,' he admitted. 'The way things are at the minute, it's very, very difficult to adopt children. There is so much red tape to get through.

'I always imagined, even when I was younger, that I would have a family of my own one day and it hurts to think that may not happen. My view on the whole thing is that kids do need to be brought up in a very safe, secure and loving home. But I definitely think there are gay couples out there who are as good parents as straight ones. You never know what will happen in the future. I feel I would have missed out a big part of life if I didn't have kids. [But] I'm happier than I have ever been now. I feel so safe and secure with Andy. We have a normal relationship like anyone else. Sometimes we argue about silly things, but most of the time we get on great. I think people see a gay couple and think they must have a weird kind of relationship, but we're just like our friends who are in straight relationships.'

He and Andrew went on to become guests at another high-profile civil partnership between Matt Lucas and Kevin McGee in 2006, in which everyone dressed as pantomime characters.

And there was another reason why Stephen and

Andrew were dropping their ideas about adopting. The unpleasant brush with homophobia allied to a great deal of negative comment in the press about celebrity adoptions was making Stephen think twice: the public had shown that it was ready for a gay member of a boy band, but would this be a step too far? 'The controversy over Madonna adopting has put us off it,' he admitted. 'By us doing that, we would be opening ourselves up to criticism by adopting in the public eye – especially as a gay couple. But I think people need to focus on the child and the fact that Madonna's son is getting a better life and a better education.'

Instead, he was turning his thoughts to that much-mooted reunion. 'I'd love it to happen and, if it was just up to me, it would,' he revealed. 'It might happen, but I hate saying anything until it is signed and agreed on – which it isn't. It's not that some of the guys are dragging their feet, it's just trying to get five people in a room at the same time is so difficult. Two of us live in London, the other three are in Ireland and are doing other projects, but I would be quietly confident.'

And at least the rift with Ronan had been repaired. 'When we split, we were supposed to get back together a year later to do a tour and a new album and that didn't happen,' he reiterated to one interviewer. 'And I was angry that didn't happen. Ronan was too busy. If we had signed a contract to do it, we would have to do it. But we didn't, we just took each other's word to do it. But life is too short – and it takes more energy to hold a grudge than to talk, so we made up.'

It was a mature and pragmatic approach to take.

Meanwhile, Shane was also thinking back to the early days of the band. He'd had an 'in' and hadn't had to audition like the others, something he was profoundly grateful for. 'I was so lucky that I never had to enter a talent show or audition for anything,' he admitted. 'I don't know if I'd have had the bottle to do it. When Boyzone was formed, I sat behind a desk with Louis Walsh and we picked the band together, so Stephen Gately and Ronan Keating stood before us and impressed us enough to get the nod. The hardest part for me when Louis and I were auditioning for Boyzone was having to turn away so many people – you can't fill them with false hope.'

He reiterated these sentiments on a *Newstalk* radio interview with Orla Barry. 'I'd love it to happen,' he confessed. 'We are going to have a meeting next week in Dublin, the five of us, so there is a possibility. We'd all have to just agree to do it and it would have to be the right time. There would have to be a greatest hits tour, maybe a greatest hits album, and it would have to be well put together. It's not that he [Ronan] was holding it back, it was just that he was busy with his own personal stuff, and that's fair enough. If he has the time, he will probably do it.'

As he waited for the band to get its act together, Stephen's solo work carried on. He joined Ulrika Jonsson, Kay Burley, Phil Gayle, Duncan James, Clare Buckfield, Emily Symons and Lisa Scott-Lee to take part in the ITV series *Dancing On Ice*: it presented a totally different challenge from any he'd had before. In the course of the eight weeks, Jayne Torvill and Christopher Dean were training everyone, with the lowest-scoring couple being shown the door each week.

'Before I went on, I had half a bottle of whiskey and eight calming tablets,' he admitted at the end of the first week. 'If anybody had had half a Valium, I'd have had that too! I was so nervous. I'm used to crowds and that's second nature, but that's because I know how to sing. I don't know how to skate. It kind of took me by surprise how frightened I was and I can't say I actually enjoyed the performance – I looked like a rabbit caught in the headlights! But hopefully I won't be as bad this week. I really enjoy rehearsals, so I just need to conquer my fear of the audience.'

Unlike performing with Boyzone, there was also a

very good chance that he might get hurt. 'The problem is, Torvill and Dean, who coach us, make it look so simple.' He continued. 'But it's not. For the first week I was clinging on to the barrier because, when you fall, it's hard.'

There were also rumours that Clare Buckfield had had skating lessons prior to joining, much to the chagrin of everyone else. 'I read that we were all cross with her, but I haven't heard anything,' insisted Stephen indignantly. 'She's really good, but I don't think she would come on a competition where you're meant to be an amateur, if she'd had lessons. I'd be really surprised. I know it's part popularity contest as much as it's about your skating, so I keep trying to remember to smile, smile, smile – but it's hard when you're nervous!'

And he had already pulled a muscle, while his skating partner, Kristina Lenko, a Canadian ice dancer, also had a nasty fall. Stephen was generous about her. 'She's got a stunning, amazing body,' he said. 'And this week I get to spank her bottom in our routine. A lot of men are going to be very jealous, but it's a bit wasted on me!'

Kristina had her own problems: while the show was going out, she was in the process of getting divorced from Steven Cousins, the eight-times British skating champion. She was attempting to put it behind her, though, and concentrate on her work with the other Stephen. 'I don't trust him yet,' she admitted. 'I'm getting there and he's still learning. Stephen picks me up and I can feel him rock back and forward on his skates. It's unnerving, but you have to remember that these celebrities have only been skating for weeks. They're doing moves you don't really do until you've had five years of training. The whole nature of the show is to push and challenge the stars to do dramatic moves. There is always an element of risk and everyone loves it when they see people fall – it's part of the fun.'

The judges and their frequently barbed comments were also part of the entertainment, especially Jason Gardiner. Kristina stood up for him. 'Jason's not half as nasty as he makes out, but it makes for great entertainment when he gets harsh with people,' she said. 'But it's hard for the celebrities as it can make them feel insecure. And you have to be confident to go out there on the ice.'

And Jason certainly didn't pull any punches when it came to Stephen. 'I choreographed Stephen and have immense respect for him for coming out,' he said. 'He's a sweet, almost innocent thing, like a kitten. But the only way he'll win is if all the others break both their legs.'

It made for fine old entertainment, though, with a

row even breaking out about how and when to use the show's fake tan.

But skating wasn't the only thing on Stephen's mind: he was also venturing into children's literature and had started work on a book. 'I haven't even got a publisher yet, but I am writing it for me,' he revealed. 'It's called *The Three Seasons* and I am putting everything into it. No ghost writers or anything. It is very Harry Potter-esque, three kids on a magical mission to save the world. There is a wicked witch, but I don't want to reveal who she is.'

But, despite all this activity, there was one project that Stephen couldn't keep his mind off – the reunion that everyone had been talking about for so long.

CHAPTER THIRTEEN

A REUNION —
OR NOT?

Stephen continued to occupy himself with *Dancing On Ice*, although talks about a forthcoming tour were becoming more positive now. On the show, meanwhile, his lack of height and slight frame caused the odd problem. 'He is only 5ft 4in, the same height as her [Kristina],' said one insider. 'This is their most difficult routine. She is understandably nervous – she does not feel safe dancing with him.'

Kristina herself admitted, 'We will never do really big lifts, so we will focus on Stephen's strengths,' while Stephen added, 'My dancing skills come into play now. What I lack in lifts, we are trying to make up in routine.'

Ultimately, he was to leave in early February, after a skate-off against the footballer Lee Sharpe. And he intended to continue skating, however: 'They've asked me to do the *Dancing On Ice* tour,' he revealed. 'I've not said yes, yet. But lots of things happen. We'll see.'

Of course, it was a very different tour that was really on his mind. 'If we do this tour, the comeback is going to have to be in Dublin, to start with,' he told one interviewer. 'It wouldn't seem right anywhere else. The lads have all said they would want the first night to be on stage in front of a home crowd; it would be an amazing way to come back. We'd have to try and find a suitable venue because we'd want a really big crowd there. To be honest, if we could just do one massive show for the Irish fans that would be a dream come true.

'If people outside Ireland bought tickets for other gigs too, that would be a bonus. I've always felt that we ended the band too early and it would be nice to see if we still have the magic. There was nothing as amazing as the feeling of being on stage at a Boyzone show. Our fans were really incredible. I'd love to experience that feeling for even one last time just to really enjoy it and make the most of it. The rest of the lads are really up for this, so I hope it will happen this time.'

The plans began to take substance. As had been previously hinted at, a greatest hits album and accompanying tour seemed to be the best way forward: 'Everybody is on board and they met record bosses to thrash out the finer details,' said an industry insider. 'They decided to go with Universal because they already hold Boyzone's back catalogue. They also saw what a fantastic job they did with Take That and hope they can have similar success. Everybody is really excited. They only agreed to do it if all five of them and their ex-manager Louis Walsh were in on it. They have had their arguments in the past, but things have moved on now and they are all getting on better than ever.'

According to Stephen, arranging the tour was turning into one giant party. 'We can't get anything planned because we always end up getting drunk together,' he said. 'We all get on so well that, as soon as we meet, the Guinness is flowing and things get out of hand. It's a hell of a party, but the whole planning process suffers. We are meant to be discussing gigs and albums, and we end up having a big singsong. There are always rotten hangovers the next day and then we all get on with our own plans. The comeback is definitely going to happen, but we need to keep away from the pub!'

Louis was thoroughly enjoying bringing the band back together, too, and revealed the secret of how they came by their name. 'I was looking for a name for the band one night,' he said. 'I was walking down Soho. I was looking in a very dodgy sex shop and I saw this video and I saw "Boyzone" on it – that's where I got the name.'

It might have been a shocker for some of the younger fans, but no one seemed to mind. But, with the comeback, other duties came to the fore, not least the fact that years had passed since they had been on stage together and it was time to get their act together again. This meant hitting the gym. 'They had preliminary talks with the management company and they have told the lads they are dreadfully out of shape,' said a source close to the band. 'They have been ordered to go on serious diets and get in the gym before they can make the comeback. Most of the Boyzone lads are in their thirties now and they aren't in the same shape they used to be. The lads were pretty surprised, but they've agreed to get top personal trainers and get back in great shape. The last thing they want is to have a new single out and they have to hold their bellies in at the photo-shoots. Take That also had to undergo a huge image revamp when they came back – they spent a month in the gym before they launched their first single.'

Work was also beginning on the greatest hits album, which would also feature two new tracks. 'We are flying to LA to record the two new tracks,' said

Keith in March 2007. 'Once that is done, we hope that we can release it ahead of Christmas and then Boyzone are back. It will be great to get into the studio again. The deal is practically done, there are a few creases to iron out, but that's the plan.'

Even now, however, Ronan was being a little bit coy, hinting that it might just be the one-off rather than a tour. 'I'm definitely up for doing something, but it's difficult enough to get the time,' he remarked. 'At this stage we are more likely to do one big show rather than loads of gigs. I have an album coming out and will be touring and promoting it, so that will be my priority.'

There was nothing the boys could do but wait and hope. 'All the lads are realistic about what Ronan can do,' a source commented. 'They know he has a solo career and is already committed to releasing a new album and touring with it. Ronan has never stood in their way of pursuing their own careers, so there has to be a level of mutual respect. He has been very upfront and honest about his commitments, so the lads are all very understanding. But the bottom line is the big tour that was originally planned is now unlikely. It's a matter of Ronan and the rest of the lads agreeing on a date for a one-off show now.'

Stephen was certainly keen on the reunion and he was becoming increasingly open about the distress he'd felt after the initial parting of the ways. 'I was so down and devastated for years after we broke up,' he admitted. 'It was a nightmare. The whole thing hit me really hard and I hid myself away from the world. Because of that, it would be great closure for me to be able to perform with the lads one more time. I've never made a secret of the fact that I've always wanted us to reunite and finish things properly with a big tour. I would spend nights crying and hurting and struggling to get to grips with my new life. It just felt like there was massive hole there and it took me a long time to get over it.'

The others were making plans, too. In August 2007, Shane, who had become a born-again Christian, married his girlfriend Sheena White at Kinnity Castle in Co Offaly, which was another chance for the five of them to meet up and discuss the future. Shane was philosophical about his own contribution to the band. 'As far as singing was concerned, if I did it in the shower, you were lucky! If I did it in the car on the way to work, listening to the radio, you were lucky!' he said. 'I don't think I even did that, to be honest. If you had a slight vocal talent, fair enough, you had a little bit of an edge. Generally speaking, it was how you looked and I guess I had the right look and I got in.'

There was some astonishment expressed when,

in September 2007, it emerged that Stephen quite genuinely seemed to have some form of healing power. He had long been interested in alternative therapies, especially colours and crystals, but had taken a course called Thought Field Therapy, or TFT, run by Paul McKenna, and now put it to good use.

He went to Manchester to appear in *Godspell* at the Palace Theatre and started chatting to the theatre's press officer, Zoe Graham, who suffered severe claustrophobia and had a terror of lifts. Somehow Stephen managed to cure her of this.

'It came out by such a random conversation,' revealed Zoe. 'He sat down in the theatre, when he came to do some interviews, and we were having a chat and it came up that I was terrified of lifts. He said, "I can cure you of that," and I said, "All right then." I'm mainly terrified of lifts, but, if a train goes under a tunnel for too long or a space feels enclosed, then I do get scared. It's mainly lifts that I've had a terror of for years, since I was about four or five. I actually got locked in the toilets of a department store with my grandma and we couldn't get out, that's where it all stems from. It would get to the point where I would deliberately avoid the lifts – I've been known to climb 11 flights of stairs in hotels, just to avoid lifts. I have had major panic attacks.'

Just weeks earlier, the fear had all but paralysed her. 'I had to go to London to do some interviews with one of our stars and I refused to get in the lift,' Zoe recalled. 'I ended up crying my eyes out and the concierge had to open the fire escape for me. It's annoying because it's something I can't control and I looked so stupid in front of all these professionals, crying like a baby because I can't get into the lift.

'He [Stephen] sat me down, he tapped on my neck, he tapped on my wrists, under my eyes and on my side, and asked me how afraid I was of lifts on a scale of one to 10. I said 20. He tapped me with two fingers 20 times on my wrists. He repeated this process about three times and then after that a calm feeling came over me – it's very strange to describe.'

And somehow, the technique had worked. 'I'm OK now, I'm much better,' she said. 'I have to admit, and I said this to Stephen, I will say, "OK, I have to get into this lift now," but it's not the hysterics it once was, it's just something I do now. I got into a lift last night that was quite small with some colleagues of mine and that didn't bother me as much as it used to. It has had such a positive effect.

'He told me initially he did it for himself because he got stage fright. Seeing him on stage for *Godspell*, you wouldn't think he had stage fright. He learned the technique through a course run by Paul McKenna, which how I understand it channels your energy elsewhere. Stephen worked wonders. It's really weird to get into a lift now, it's mad really. It makes you think how powerful the mind actually is, it's mind over matter. For me now it's two minutes in a lift. It really did work.

'I was very confident that it would work and I'm very pleased that I've been able to help Zoe out,' was Stephen's modest response.

He also said that he could sense the paranormal. 'When I was a kid I cleaned a theatre – I had to get up at 6am in the morning and clean the theatre for two-and-a-half hours, then go to school for 9am,' he recalled on television's *Loose Women*. 'I was only 16 and it was really haunted, so I was terrified. I've had many experiences – I had a woman in a hotel room who appeared to me once. She was tying her bonnet up and she tutted, waved her finger at me and floated out the door. Apparently, she had an argument with her husband on her wedding week – they were on their honeymoon and he locked her in a blanket case and she was scratching to get out. I heard the scratches in the room the night before.'

By the end of the year, it was finally confirmed: Boyzone were to be reunited, and it would be a proper tour, not a one-off occasion. Each of the band mates was expected to pocket at least £1 million, while they got into the swing of things by performing together for the first time in seven years for BBC's *Children in Need*. 'We've been talking about getting back together for some time now,' said Ronan. 'The *Children in Need* rehearsals just made us want to tour together again. I can't wait to be back on the road and all the guys feel the same. It's going to be an incredible buzz to go out there and perform for all the fans again.'

And there were quite a few other bands with the same idea, not least The Spice Girls. 'We've been trying to find the right moment to do this for a long time – before Take That considered it, before The Police were ever considering it,' reflected Ronan. 'I remember in one of our meetings last year we were thinking, Well, The Spice Girls aren't gonna do it 'cos two girls are pregnant. We never expected them to come back. There were quite a lot of people at the meeting and a lot of things we talked about I felt were leaked. A lot of what The Spice Girls did was what we'd talked about, so maybe there was someone in the room that spread the word, I don't know. It looks like Take That and The Spice Girls did it and we're trying to jump on the bandwagon, but it's not like that. There are about 40 shows in the UK and Ireland, then we look at Europe.'

And Louis, of course, would be involved, having

had his own rapprochement with Ronan. 'They were avoiding each other for ages,' revealed Stephen. 'Then they met one night and it was all right. There were six of us in the band in a sense. It would feel awkward if Louis wasn't there. To try to do something without him wouldn't be the same. We respect him very much.'

They were certainly older and wiser now, that much was clear, and was reinforced by an observation from Keith: 'It'll be good to experience it this time, instead of getting drunk every night and not seeing anything.'

CHAPTER FOURTEEN

THE BOYZ ARE BACK IN TOWN

As 2008 dawned, the boys were beginning to gear up to the tour with growing excitement. Stephen had one last solo role – a part in a low-budget horror flick called *Credo* – but, otherwise, he was getting ready for the role that had originally made him a star.

An initial appearance was at London's G.A.Y. club in March. It was to test the waters, as it were, and accustom the boys to being back on stage together – after all, it had been seven years. And the change in their circumstances since they had first started out, 15 years earlier, could not have been more pronounced: Ronan was out and about early the next day to take his three children to a VIP screening of *Horton Hears a Who!* No longer boys, they were men with adult responsibilities now.

Even so, it was a little overwhelming. Whatever

feuds and rows they'd had since going their separate ways, this was still where they had all come from, and where it all started. 'To be honest, as long as it feels good and we're having fun, we will continue with it,' said Mikey. 'Our plan is to tour, have a greatest hits album and a couple of new songs by the end of this year. And then there could be a new album in 2009. As far as breaking up is concerned, I don't think we'll be doing it again. We are really enjoying this a lot more than we did before.'

In some ways, of course, they'd all felt a bit stale before the break-up and wanted to try something new. And, having forged reasonably successful alternative careers, they'd all succeeded. But Boyzone remained a hugely popular band and the demand for them to come back was enormous. And, having seen that life could be a little cold outside, they were clearly immensely relieved to be back.

'I was looking into doing a reunion tour for the last two years or so,' Mikey continued. 'I am good friends with Gary Barlow and I had seen how everything happened with Take That. I went to see their show in the Point Depot and it was just one of the best shows I had ever seen, so straight away I was on the phone to Shane and subsequently the other guys, saying how it was amazing. I hadn't missed being in Boyzone at all until I got to that gig. And slowly the bridges were mended through time with the other guys and now we are up and running.

'We were very apprehensive about how we would be received; we didn't know if our fans would give us the support we had years ago. And obviously we are humbly thrilled with the response. We would love to give our fans a big thank you.'

The boys gathered in Dublin to rehearse the show, although there was a minor hiccup when Keith got blood poisoning after acquiring a new tattoo. The general consensus was that they had better be good: Take That had raised the bar so high that Boyzone would have to be singing and dancing as never before.

'Take That have set a huge challenge,' Ronan conceded. 'Their comeback was flawless and we need the same. If it's a crap show, it's easy to be pushed aside. Rehearsals are going very well: we're dancing more, singing better and are hungrier for it. It's a massive, massive production. It would have been easy to make a quick buck, but we are sinking all the money from the tour into the show itself.'

All, however, were adamant that this was not about money. 'There's no way this is about money,' said Ronan. 'We're all very well-off from our time in Boyzone. If it had been about the cash, we wouldn't have done it. I don't think any of us need the money in this group. If I'm honest, I wasn't sure anyone would even care if we came back. How wrong was I?'

'We did this for nostalgia because we wanted to remember what it was like,' Stephen added. 'Some people think we saw an opportunity to make big money, but that's not the case.'

And they were certainly pulling out all the stops. 'It's going to be spectacular,' continued Stephen. 'When we were younger we were so concerned about trying to crack the market, make our breakthrough, that we were under too much pressure to really enjoy it, but, when we did the first comeback performance on *Children in Need* last year, you could really see the smile on my face, so imagine what I'm going to be like on stage for a full show!

'There is singing practising, diet, gym, the whole shebang. And dancing classes – there will be more dancing than we have ever done before. We are getting on like a house on fire, laughing at each other as well as ourselves, and we are not being too serious about it, except when it comes to putting in the work.'

The show kicked off at Belfast's Odyssey Arena, starting with a Michael Jackson medley, naturally complete with the moonwalk. The boys had been true to their word: it was a spectacle, with dancers writhing away in the background, many and varied dance routines, special effects and, of course, all their greatest hits. Ronan was allowed to include a couple of his own, too: 'When You Say Nothing At All' and 'Life Is A Rollercoaster'. The fans absolutely adored it.

The dancers were a new touch, and inspired by Take That. According to Ronan, his wife Yvonne had encouraged him to dance with them. 'She was the one who wanted me to get stuck in,' he admitted. 'We had our fair share of fun at home testing out the moves. I admit that during the gig I didn't know where to look: our dancers are unbelievably sexy and didn't have much on. Yvonne got something out of it, too – she likes the new muscular me!'

The boys certainly had been working hard to bulk up – but they had to, given that they were topless in some segments of the show. And it was widely commented on how they really were men now, not boys, which meant that all the female attention that they received the first time around was now back in spades.

'We are getting more female attention now than ever before, it's just crazy,' said a clearly stunned Mikey. 'Boyzone never really got much attention back in the early days, but we certainly do now. More and more fans are following us around, and just last week there were over 100 fans outside a radio station in

London waiting for us to turn up. It really took us all by surprise. It can get hairy at times, but for the most part it's just a lot of fun.'

This new high profile did have some disadvantages, though: burglars broke into Stephen and Andrew's house and stole £80,000 worth of jewellery, including a custom-made Rolex watch that he'd bought with his first royalty cheque. 'I'm deeply upset because these items had great sentimental value and the reality is that they'll probably be sold off for a fraction of their true value in some second-hand shop,' he commented glumly. 'Of all the things I've lost, I'm most upset about the Rolex watch as all the boys in the band bought one as a memento with our first pay cheques when we became famous. [But] I really love Highgate and wouldn't move away for the world. It has a great vibe and the people here are brilliant.'

It was not, strangely enough, the only problem with theft that Stephen had back then. At around the same time, someone got hold of his credit card details and ran up a £20,000 bill before he found out. 'Stephen is starting to think he is cursed,' revealed a friend. 'He has no idea how this fraudster got hold of his card details. When he checked over the statement, there were penthouse hotel suites, flights and even holidays to locations all around the world; there were also cash withdrawals in four different countries. Someone was living the high life off his card for months. They are trying to track down the culprit and now Stephen has to apply to get his money back.'

At least the tour was going well. Occasionally, Ronan would mention the band's split when they were on stage, provoking boos from the crowd: he was, he conceded, the villain of the piece. 'I have never been forgiven for that in Ireland and I probably never will be,' he said. 'All I can say is that we all made mistakes around that time, myself included. We all have some responsibility for what happened and I certainly share in that. We all wanted to take a break, but I was the one who made it permanent.'

But Ireland was certainly revelling in them now. The boys made a return to Gay Byrne's *The Late, Late Show* to perform their comeback single, 'Love You Anyway' – this was the show on which they had had such a catastrophic debut all those years before. Their performance this time was flawless.

In October, Shane became a father when his wife Sheena gave birth to a daughter, Billie Rae. 'I'm absolutely thrilled,' he said. 'It's a true gift from God and I am so in awe of Sheena. She did fantastically well and it was the most emotional experience of my life; I feel like the luckiest man alive. I want to thank everyone who has sent me messages of congratulations and we can't wait to bring the baby home now and start life as a little family.'

Of course, his fellow band mates were thrilled for him but it did mean that Stephen was the only member of Boyzone now without a child. But he knew by then that it was never going to happen. He still got the odd homophobic remark tossed in his direction and didn't want to give any more ammunition to the critics – although, in fact, the whole band was about to do just that.

Indeed, they were about to make pop music history, but, just before they did so, they found themselves in a situation more suited to their much younger days, when they ended up in a punch-up in Sydney. The boys went out on a bender with their old friend Brian McFadden, now living in the city, when they encountered R & B star Rihanna and her entourage. Someone started chatting up one of the girls. 'Her boyfriend took offence and all hell broke loose, with fists flying everywhere,' said a witness to the scene. 'Despite being a little unsteady on their feet, the boys more than held their own in the fracas, but it wasn't long before security came racing over and broke it all up. They were given a stern talking-to.'

And they sounded more than a little sheepish in the wake of events. 'Well, we did get into a fight, maybe more of an altercation, but certainly more than a difference of opinion,' Stephen conceded. 'We are just keeping up that fine image of the Irish and too much booze. We feel it fits right in with Aussies. It was over one of Rihanna's band members' girlfriends – we just wanted to chat and be friendly, and suddenly this guy starts trying to rough us up. It was his girl and then all the other guys from the band start getting fresh with us, so it was on there and then.'

Ronan laughed it off. 'He [Brian] completely lead us astray,' he said. 'Blame him! He knows all the nasty haunts in this city. We are the ones usually leading him into evil, back home, so this time the tables were turned.'

It was a rare moment of controversy in an otherwise highly productive time for the boys and they were about to hit the headlines again. As the success of the tour began to make itself felt, it was clear that there was a market for new material, and so towards the end of the year, Boyzone released a new single, 'Better'. It was a love song, and Stephen, having been the first member of a boy band to come out, chalked up another first: he became part of a gay couple in the video. It showed all the members of Boyzone with partners but Stephen's opposite number was played by a man.

'For me, it's just me being me and I don't think

there should be a real big issue about the whole thing,' said Stephen. 'I just think it's just a beautiful video and I think it works superbly for the song. I'm hoping this video will have a good, positive, all-round reaction. I don't think I could have done it without having a guy in it – it's important for me to be true to myself. The lads were saying, "You've got to do this, it would be fantastic." It's the first of its kind and that's why I went for it.'

It must be said that the other members of Boyzone had never been anything other than utterly supportive of Stephen, and this was quite a step for a group of young, working-class Dubliners to take. But it certainly didn't garner universal support: Ireland was still a conservative country and it did not go down well at all.

'It's another effort of the homosexual propaganda machine,' said the Presbyterian Reverend David McCullough. 'It's stating that homosexuality is the norm. The message from God is very different: homosexual desires and behaviour are a clear violation of God's law. God made Adam and Eve, not Adam and Steve.'

Stephen was outraged. 'This guy doesn't know the same God that I do!' he declared. 'The rest of the Boyzone lads were completely in support of me over this video. I was being true to myself and this is the first time anyone has said anything negative about my appearance in the video. I go to church, I pray and the fact that one in every ten people is gay shows that God obviously doesn't have the same view about homosexual people as David McCullough.

'It would have been more ridiculous if I appeared in the video with a woman since all our fans have known I'm gay for nearly ten years! I would welcome this man to come to any of our concerts and see how many church-going people enjoy them. It's a shame that he could be using his time to promote the beauty of Christianity and instead he is ranting on about negative issues that really aren't that important in the grand scheme of things.'

Ronan defended their actions, too – after all, the video was sanctioned by the whole band. 'It's unbelievable for someone in their position to say things like that,' he said. 'It's understandable that they may have been brought up to think like that, but such negative comments are really just not helpful in this day and age. We all supported Stephen's choice to have a male dancer – all the fuss has been absolutely ridiculous. I really hope someone in the Church got their knuckles severely rapped for this.'

Keith also spoke out. 'He's living in medieval times with his attitude, unbelievable! If these guys were so verbal when their own kind are caught doing things they shouldn't be doing... It's only when innocent little boy bands like Boyzone are honest to their fans they start kicking up a fuss!'

But Boyzone had certainly made history. That, as much as the music, will be Stephen's legacy.

CHAPTER FIFTEEN

FAREWELL TO STEPHEN

There was nothing to indicate that 2009 would be Stephen Gately's last year on earth. Quite the opposite, in fact: things had looked up professionally, he was happy in his private life and neither he nor anyone else knew that he was suffering from ill health. Indeed, it seemed that the only way was up.

Stephen certainly seemed the fittest of the lot of them. 'When he goes into the gym and lifts heavier than I can, I'm a bit embarrassed,' admitted Shane. 'This guy trains more than any of us. He's a bloody psycho when it comes to being in a gym!'

And Stephen – along with everyone else – was delighted that the comeback had gone so well. The initial parting had been traumatic, but now he had his old life back. 'I was depressed for a while [after the break-up],' he said. 'I just became a bit paranoid and had to take medication. It was only when I got the part in *Joseph* that I could pull myself out of that dark hole.'

Even Ronan had found it colder on the outside than he had previously admitted. 'I came out of Boyzone, had a massive album and it was like I was on a wave,' he recalled. 'My second album was fantastic and then the third album slowed down. And the fourth album did, too, and it hurt. It's not nice for your self-esteem, but I think it's healthy because it makes you appreciate what you had.'

But now they had it back and all the old rivalries and tensions were gone: they had grown up and knew that it would be madness to throw away a second chance. 'There were constant ego battles, but we're not jockeying for position any more,' said Stephen. 'We have a golden opportunity and we're grabbing it with both hands.'

'Nowadays we push Ronan – our best asset – forward, because we want what's best for the band,' added Keith.

'When we get together now, we're like five kids again,' said Mikey. 'I feel guilty sometimes about the amount of fun we have – we're lucky to be in a position to have a job that's such fun.'

'We've a lot of things that keep our feet on the

ground and our families have been incredibly important,' continued Ronan. 'We now have things in our life that are more crucial than the band.'

And Stephen was certainly relaxed about his sexuality. 'It is now me being myself,' he said. 'Before I told anyone I was gay, it got me down a bit. I think Louis Walsh would still have picked me for the band if he had known that I was gay, even though he has said otherwise, but that's just Louis being Louis. I was meant to be the cute one! Nowadays there seems to be a new criteria – let's get a gay one.'

He had, however, enjoyed *not* being the cute one in *Credo*. 'I had to lie in a pool of blood for about three-and-a-half hours – which was fantastic – and just turn over and not be able to breathe or blink for about a minute,' he revealed. 'It's great to look at yourself in the mirror with your throat slashed, with the make-up done, looking all gaunt. People do say I'm the cute one in Boyzone – I think this gives the perfect opportunity to show people I'm not.'

Stephen's influence was felt by the band in other ways: now they were all very keen to look after themselves. 'After their first show in Belfast on Sunday night, they will have a team of local beauticians coming to the hotel to look after them,' said a source close to the band. 'All the lads will get massages and a few of them have even booked facials.

Stephen is always trying to encourage the lads to look after their skin and keep their youthful looks, and they are all into it. They are eating better, drinking less and they have all become very metrosexual.'

And there were very light-hearted sides to it all, too. The band had had to invest in specially reinforced trousers, as they kept splitting their own. 'From pretty much the first night, we kept splitting some trousers and it was actually quite entertaining, particularly when you've got no arse,' said Shane. 'We all managed to split the trousers in one night because we get them really tightly made. It's all well and good until you get on stage and are dancing flat out. You don't realise the silk they are made from is not that robust, so we had to get them altered to take the pressure – right where it counts!'

And, like the rest of them, he was thoroughly enjoying himself. 'We've been on the road pretty much since 20 May and it's been a good few weeks,' he continued. 'The show is awesome. Last year, when we came back, we put on a really good show and we didn't know how we could make it better this time, but we flipped it up a little bit and changed some of the clothing and stuff. The fans have changed in some respects and it is amazing: they have bottles of beer and glasses of wine. Before we came back on tour, we always thought it would be a little more reserved audience because they were more mature, but they are even worse than before; they are wild!'

Something else had happened behind the scenes, too. In an interview he gave shortly before his death, Stephen revealed that he had finally healed the rift with his parents. 'It was crazy because you need your family and I isolated myself,' he admitted. Indeed, he and Andrew had gone to visit them in the old family home in Sheriff Street. 'It was so nostalgic and quite emotional,' Stephen went on. 'It was a lovely experience. They [his parents] are still very happy there.'

Stephen's sudden and unexpected death, at a time when he had everything to live for, shocked the world. In death, Boyzone reclaimed him as one of their own, just as they had done in the two years that they had together when the band re-formed. All have been striving to keep his memory alive; all have been shocked to the core.

The rest of the band made the decision to stay together in the wake of Stephen's death and to record a new album, incorporating vocals that were recorded by him shortly before he died. 'We have decided we're going to make the next album for Stephen,' announced Ronan. 'We're going to go forward as Boyzone and we're going to make this new record.

We'd like to do that as soon as possible because we have individual things that we have to go and do, but we don't want to be apart; we find comfort in being together at the moment.

'We have a couple of songs with Stephen's vocal on it, so that's a saving grace; thank God we have that. That's very important to all of us and we know the fans would really appreciate that too, so that's what we're going to do. I hope we can keep his memory alive. In all the years I knew Steo, I've never seen him as radiant, as happy, as healthy, as strong, as confident, as comfortable in his own skin, and that's what's really difficult for all of us.'

In fact, Ronan and Stephen's last contact was the night that Stephen died. 'Just before he was going out on the Friday night, he just sent me a text, so excited about the album,' he remembered. 'He sent me, "Love you straw balls, speak soon". I can't tell you what I texted back. That's the way we were, we were great pals.'

Ronan was, in fact, knocked for six by the death of his friend. As the *de facto* spokesman for the band, it was perhaps natural that he would be the one to enunciate all their feelings, but his grief was so raw that it made uncomfortable viewing. 'I just don't understand it,' he mused. 'Why has he gone, why was he taken? I question my faith constantly, but I'm a believer so I try to think there must be some sort of logic behind it, that God wanted him.

'I don't think I will ever get over this. I miss him every day – I've never cried so much in my life. All I wanted to do was crawl into a ball. I've got no tears left, I'm totally drained of all emotion, I am numb. I've never known anything like this, not even the death of my own mother.'

Of course, Stephen was so young and so vibrant. It was scarcely believable that he had died with so much to live for and so much ahead.

Ronan had known for a while that his mother was going to die, but he did not have that same time to prepare himself when it came to his friend. 'I've never before thought about going to get help with counsellors,' he said. 'For the first time ever, I think I should. When I lost my mum, it was the hardest thing at the time I'd ever known in my life, but because she was sick for two years and we were told three months before she died that she had three months [left], subconsciously you build a wall, your defence mechanism goes up and you prepare yourself for that. Whereas, with Steo, there was nothing, just this wall of devastation, shock. I don't think it has hit any of us properly. There's times when you feel like you can't breathe, you know, when you're panicking and I'm not like that. I've always been on a level.'

He still wanted to talk about Stephen, though, as the bereaved so often do: it keeps the person they have lost alive. 'I didn't see his body until we got back to Dublin,' he recalled. 'The first time we saw him was in the funeral home. That was very hard, the hardest thing I've ever done; I knew I had to see him. Everybody has their own way, but I knew I had to say goodbye. We went in together with our wives and partners, and I spoke to him.

'I was shaking, I almost collapsed – I had to hold on to the wall. What I said is between me and Steo but I said my goodbye. That night we brought him down to the church and we carried him in and the priest said a few words, and then everybody left and the four of us spent the night in sleeping bags on the floor beside him. He didn't like the dark and his mum didn't want him being in the church on his own, so we said we'd spend the night with him. It was our last night as a five-piece. I got about an hour-and-a-half's sleep. We sat up talking and laughing and crying, and telling stories and, every so often, someone would call out, "Yeah, Steo – what do you think of that?"'

Ronan also wanted to defend the memory of his friend, especially and above all when it came to the lurid speculation surrounding Georgi Dochev, the Bulgarian who had been present on the night of

Stephen's death. 'I don't know him, but he was a friend of Stephen and Andrew's,' said Ronan. 'They had known him for a while. There was absolutely nothing going on between him and Andrew.'

He then addressed the subject of drink and drugs. 'Steo was one of the healthiest guys I knew,' he said. 'He had a drink – we all had a drink – but he wasn't one of those people who would binge drink or drink all the time. It was a freak accident.'

Ronan also looked back on when he heard the news from Gerald Kean. 'I'll never forget that call,' he said. 'He said, "Hello, Ronan, I have some bad news. Stephen's passed away." Not for one second did I imagine it was Steo. So I said, "Stephen *who*?" And he said, "Stephen Gately."

'I was in hysterics and I couldn't calm myself down. I called Andrew straight away. I said, "Please tell me it's not true," and he said, "I'm sorry, it's not good." I called my wife Yvonne and then the three boys; I didn't want them to hear it from anyone else. Every time I rang the lads and said the words I just broke down again. I was devastated.'

And then, of course, the boys had all travelled to Majorca. 'We needed to be together and to be with Andrew,' continued Ronan. 'We went straight to the apartment and just sat with Andrew and listened to him as he told us basically what had happened. And then, after all the tears, we started to talk about getting him home.'

It was Boyzone themselves who made all the funeral arrangements – after all, who had been closer to Stephen than them? 'It helped me greatly and gave me a focus,' admitted Ronan. 'I knew what Stephen wanted and I tried to make that happen. We all knew what we had to do and that was bring Stephen back – we didn't want him to be on his own.'

But that was distressing, too, when they even had to make the choice of coffin. 'I'll never forget it,' said Ronan. 'My legs were weak, collapsing – I had to grab the wall as I went into the room. It was like a showroom with coffins in it, you know? I mean, you pick a coffin, for fuck's sake! I couldn't make head nor tail of it, my legs went from under me and I was just weak.'

Another factor in bereavement is bitter regret about past mistakes. Stephen had been very open about the fact that the break-up of the band had caused him to suffer from depression and now Ronan appeared to be blaming himself about that, too. 'I struggle with the fact we were apart for those seven years and we didn't talk as much and I blame myself, but I'm so grateful we had those three years when the band was back together,' he admitted. 'It meant so much to Steo, so that is a saving grace.'

Ronan had a new album out called *Winter Songs*, which also featured Stephen on the track 'Little Drummer Boy'. 'Three weeks ago, I had no interest in going back to work and promoting this record, but that's one of the reasons I have come back because I know he's on the record and I want people to hear,' he said. 'It's his last proper studio recording. I've listened to it a thousand times since he passed away.'

And so, in song, at least, the boys would always be together. Stephen Gately came from the backstreets of Dublin, a working-class boy who went on to pull down barriers and make show-business history. It had ended much too soon – but, all in all, what a life it had been.